THE STINKING ROSE
RESTAURANT
Cookbook

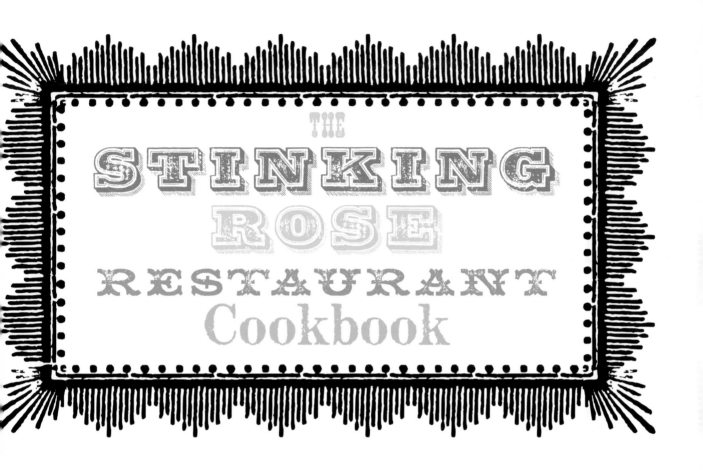

THE STINKING ROSE RESTAURANT Cookbook

BY Andrea Froncillo WITH Jennifer Jeffrey

PHOTOGRAPHY BY Caren Alpert

TEN SPEED PRESS

Berkeley

Library of Congress Cataloging-in-Publication Data
Froncillo, Andrea.
   The Stinking Rose Restaurant cookbook / by Andrea Froncillo,
   with Jennifer Jeffrey ; photography by Caren Alpert.
      p. cm.
      Includes index.
         1. Cookery, American—California style. 2. Cookery (Garlic)
      3. Stinking Rose (Restaurant) I. Jeffrey, Jennifer. II. Title.
   TX715.2.C34.F76 2006
      641.'526—dc22   2005037315

ISBN: 978-1-58008-686-8 (hardcover)

Printed in China

Front cover photograph © by Johner Images / Getty Images
Jacket design by Betsy Stromberg and Kate Basart/Union Pageworks
Text design by Kate Basart/Union Pageworks
Food styling by Robyn Valarik
Prop styling by Jeneffer Jones Rosen
Photography assistance by Dylan Maddux
Select props courtesy Sur La Table, Inc., www.surlatable.com

13 12 11 10 9 8 7 6 5

First Edition

CONTENTS

WELCOME

I am so glad you stopped by! My name is Andrea Froncillo, and I'm the executive chef here at the Stinking Rose. Step inside and let me show you around! As you can see, the restaurant looks like a stage set for a movie. The walls are festooned with bulbs of garlic and plastered with pictures of Italian film stars, celebrities, and personalities; the ceiling drips with a dazzling array of chandeliers; the tables are covered with bright ceramic dishes and wax-encrusted candlesticks; the sounds of Frank Sinatra and Ella Fitzgerald and Dean Martin float above the hum and clatter. Through it all wafts the distinctive aroma of garlic.

Legend has it that the Romans first called garlic the "stinking rose," and we match its intense aroma and flavor in every way, with over-the-top decor, generous portions, and festive ambience. We've got big bulbs, and we're not shy about showing them off. From the pungent Rose Relish that we bring to every table with a basket of freshly baked garlic buns to our famous Garlic-Roasted Killer Crab, our menu is an enthusiastic celebration of taste and texture. Hey, life is short! Why not grab it with both hands and shake every bit of stinky goodness out of it?

Whether or not you've ever been inside the Stinking Rose, you're in for a treat in the pages that follow: I'll tell you the story of how the restaurant came to be, give you a glimpse of the rooms and booths and memorabilia that make this place special, and even take you behind the scenes to the kitchen for a peek at who and what turns this place into a party every single day. We're going to have a blast together.

Hey, what are we waiting for? Let's get started already.

FOLLOW YOUR NOSE TO THE STINKING ROSE

nce upon a time, there was a long, wide street that ran straight through the bustling city of San Francisco, from the sparking bay into the heart of downtown. Its close proximity to the port made it a thoroughfare for travelers from all over the world, and thousands of people made their way down its broad corridor as they ventured into other parts of California and beyond. It was a rough, rowdy street, crowded with sailors and hookers and hawkers of all kinds. Opportunity and mischief lurked around every corner, and more than one gullible sailor lost his hard-earned paycheck in one of its shadowy recesses.

The street was called Columbus Avenue, as it still is today, and Italian immigrants felt right at home amid its hustle and bustle. We Italians thrive in action-packed environments, and besides, the street itself was named for that most famous Italian explorer of them all, our man Christopher, and so it wasn't any surprise that we quickly claimed it as *our* neighborhood. Legend has it that during the devastating earthquake of 1906, Italian American residents hauled barrels of red wine from their cellars and soaked blankets in the wine, draping them over their houses and thereby protecting them from the fire. Let that be a lesson to you: quick thinking and a barrel of red wine *always* saves the day!

Today, Columbus Avenue is the soul of North Beach, San Francisco's version of Little Italy. First-time visitors always ask where the beach is, but they soon forget the question, as they're absorbed into the lively cafes, crowded shops, and rustic Italian markets.

Let's take a brief stroll around to get our bearings. We'll start with a familiar landmark, Coit Tower, which perches atop Telegraph Hill on the east edge of the neighborhood. The tower was named after Lillie Hitchcock Coit, an eccentric local who loved firefighters so much that one of the local units made her an honorary member. Coit Tower resembles a giant fire hose, and it is brilliantly lit up at night, towering over North Beach with a radiant glow. Residents who have had a bit much to drink have been known to use the tower as a navigational symbol to make their way back home. Or so we've heard.

If we head due north, toward the ocean and Fisherman's Wharf, we'll bump into SS Peter and Paul Church, a magnificent cathedral replete with intricate spires and carvings, hovering on the edge of Washington Square Park. This church used to be a haven for Italian fisherman, and even now it is a cherished spiritual and cultural landmark. Every October, a procession winds from the church down to Fisherman's Wharf for the annual blessing of the fishing fleet. The famous photograph of Joe DiMaggio and Marilyn Monroe was taken here, snapped just after their city hall wedding in 1954. The two weren't allowed to be married in the church, since they were both divorced, but it was important to them to have their picture taken there in spite of it.

If we turn around and head back toward downtown, we'll find another vibrant district nestled up against the south side of the neighborhood: Chinatown. Here you'll see live fish swimming around in barrels of water, baskets full of dried roots and herbs, and funky mushrooms and squiggly things in glass jars. From certain vantage points, the two communities blur into a kind of international bazaar, abuzz with people and goods and food. Here at the Stinking Rose, we've experimented with fusing some of the flavors of these two neighborhoods together, with surprisingly tasty results. Check out our Italian Pot Stickers on page 15 for a great example of Asian and Italian fusion.

But let's not stray too far from Columbus Avenue. Here, in the shadow of the Transamerica Pyramid, is where artists and intellectuals congregated during the fifties and sixties, quaffing cups of strong espresso and cheap bottles of wine while they dreamed and wrote and argued. During those same years, an upstart newspaper columnist named Herb Caen was making a name for himself as the definitive voice of San Francisco. In 1958, Herb coined the term *beatnik* in reference to the bad-boy poets and writers who made their home in North Beach, including Jack Kerouac, Allen Ginsberg, and William S. Burroughs. The nickname stuck, and Herb's legendary status kept on growing. His columns, laced with equal parts gossip, opinion, and information, were read around the world, and his droll observations became

synonymous with the City by the Bay. The City Lights Bookstore on the corner of Columbus and Broadway is a monument to those crazy days when the Beat generation roamed the streets. This landmark for writers and literary buffs was founded by Lawrence Ferlinghetti in 1953, and is still a popular gathering spot today.

But where is that amazing smell coming from? Just turn and look up the street, toward the bay, to find the source. Everyone likes to imagine that they're the center of the universe, but the Stinking Rose truly is positioned smack in the middle of it all, sending the tantalizing scent of garlic wafting through the air. It plays host to visitors from all over the globe and a good many celebrities, too. The restaurant is also a favorite with the locals. More than one love-struck boy has asked for the hand of his girl on the romantic balcony of the Stinking Rose, and many families have celebrated birthdays, weddings, and anniversaries in one of our marvelously decorated rooms.

A Long Time Ago . . .

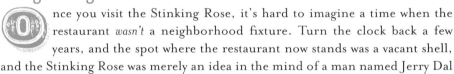 nce you visit the Stinking Rose, it's hard to imagine a time when the restaurant *wasn't* a neighborhood fixture. Turn the clock back a few years, and the spot where the restaurant now stands was a vacant shell, and the Stinking Rose was merely an idea in the mind of a man named Jerry Dal Bozzo.

Jerry Dal Bozzo was born into a first-generation Italian American family on Telegraph Hill. North Beach was his playground, and he made good use of it from the start. In high school, he and a couple of buddies organized disco dances for their classmates, parties that people talked about for days afterward. As high school drew to a close, Jerry thought about what he would do after graduation. Wouldn't it be great, he dreamed, to own a little bar or restaurant where all of his friends could keep on partying? It sure would beat a boring old office job.

Before long, Jerry became the proud proprietor of a bar on Market Street called the Gold Room. The bar was located in the old Fox Theatre, and he decorated it to look like a plush, swanky cabaret. The next task was finding someone

to play the piano, and Jerry brought in the best talent in the city, including a handsome young man named Ed Rosero. Ed's long, nimble fingers smoked up the ivories until the wee hours of the morning, and soon the place was packed.

For the next twenty years, Jerry opened various restaurants and bars throughout the city. He had a knack for picking out good properties, but his real skill was knowing how to fix up an interior that made people want to come inside . . . and stay. "I've made every mistake in the book," he grins, "and I've even invented a few."

In the mideighties, Jerry was elected president of the North Beach Chamber of Commerce, which undertook a project to clean up the neighborhood. They cleaned the sidewalks, removed unsightly graffiti, and repainted the hydrants. They posted notes that prohibited the posting of printed bulletins, and repainted the wooden light poles in red, white, and green, the colors of the Italian flag. All of their efforts paid off; the word soon got around that North Beach had cleaned up its act, and locals flooded back to the streets.

All the while, a prime spot on Columbus Avenue stood vacant. In years past, the property had played host to Little Joe's and Café American, but they had long since closed, and its windows were boarded up, making an unsightly blemish on an otherwise vibrant block. Jerry told several people about his idea for the perfect restaurant to occupy the space.

"You should open a place dedicated to garlic," he urged a couple of his restaurant buddies. "I'll even give you a perfect name: the Stinking Rose! It's a brilliant idea!"

But no one would take the bait. Finally, in 1991, restaurateur Dante Serafini convinced Jerry that they should do it together. The night the Stinking Rose opened, the place was jam-packed. It was different than any other eatery in the city: the decor was outrageous, the portions were huge, and, even better, it felt like a party inside. In the early days, the dishes were laden with garlic. Even garlic fanatics reeled as they headed for the door. The hostesses passed out mints by the bucketful, but Jerry and Dante soon realized that garlic was best delivered in small, subtle quantities. A graceful hint was all that was needed. Anything else, and the customers would be tempted to take long breaks before coming back.

For the few die-hard garlic lovers, they invented Rose Relish: a concoction of minced raw garlic blended with olive oil and chopped parsley. They placed it at the table so that true aficionados could always add more if they wanted. For the rest of the dishes, they cut back on the clove count considerably.

Bagna Calda was another early favorite. Cloves of garlic were roasted until they achieved caramely sweetness, then added to a bath of melted butter and olive oil with the barest hint of anchovies. The result was a delicious, savory treat that people sopped up on house buns just as fast as it came out of the kitchen. Bagna Calda is still a much-loved dish on the menu today.

And the Stars Come Knocking

Not surprisingly, the flamboyant interior and larger-than-life props made the restaurant a popular spot with visitors from Los Angeles during the early years. The Stinking Rose was a Hollywoodesque tribute to garlic, a fact that did not go unnoticed by Angelenos. "The most popular restaurant in L.A.," someone remarked, "is the Stinking Rose in San Francisco!" And so, in 1995, a second Stinking Rose was opened in Beverly Hills, right in the middle of showbiz central, at La Cienega and Wilshire Boulevard. The Beverly Hills location quickly attracted a celebrity following. Heather Locklear was one of the earliest fans; Heather loves garlic, and her special favorite is our Caesar salad. Countless stars have thrown birthday parties and celebrations in one of the colorful rooms, and many regularly stop by to sit at the Gar-Bar. Tony Bennett, Shaquille O'Neal, and Dr. Dre are just a few of the people who regularly stop by to indulge in Forty-Clove Garlic Chicken, Juicy Slow-Roasted Prime Rib, and Garlic-Encrusted Baby Back Ribs.

Chef Andrea Froncillo joined Jerry and Dante in 1996, adding his signature flair to the restaurants. He learned to cook from his *nonna* in the slums of Napoli, and from those early experiments with simple, basic foods came an apprecia-

tion for the sensuality of texture, presentation, and fragrance. He revamped the Stinking Rose menu to include sizzling iron skillets heaped with mussels and shrimp, and developed a recipe that he called Killer Crab, made with a secret sauce that keeps people coming back for more. Andrea continues to think up unique recipes to delight patrons, believing that food should be an adventure.

Midway through the first decade of the twenty-first century, the Stinking Rose is better than ever. New memorabilia is added frequently, and the menu is a continual rotation of scrumptious, mouthwatering delights, all enhanced by its namesake bulb.

Hungry yet?

A QUICK GUIDE TO GARLIC

Like a good woman, garlic must be pampered and cared for in order to stay in top shape. Before you launch into the recipes in this book, we recommend that you read through these tips on how to purchase, store, and cook with garlic.

Purchasing Garlic

When purchasing garlic, be sure to squeeze the bulbs before you buy. Be shameless: squeeze away until you find a bulb that is firm and hard, with no soft spots or brown marks. The skin should be papery and dry. Do not purchase garlic with any visible sprouts or sprout buds.

There are many different kinds of garlic; make it a point to stop by your local farmers' market and find out which varieties are local to you and their different flavor characteristics. Not all garlic tastes the same!

Storing Garlic

Store garlic in a cool, dry place with plenty of ventilation, away from moisture and light. A basket, a mesh bag, or a clay pot with holes all make good storage containers. Do not store garlic in the refrigerator or in a plastic bag or container. Do not store raw garlic in olive oil, as it can release compounds that are highly toxic. Discard any garlic that is soft or spotted or has begun to sprout. Keep garlic away from foods that might absorb its odor, such as fruit and potatoes.

Cooking with Garlic

To quickly remove the papery skin from a clove of garlic, place the clove flat side down on a cutting board. Lay the broad edge of a knife over the garlic and press down with the heel of your hand. You will hear a cracking sound. Release the pressure; the skin will now slide off easily. To peel a large number of cloves, drop

them into boiling water for 30 seconds. When you remove them from the water, the skins will slide off smoothly.

Many recipes in this book will direct you to sauté garlic that has been minced, chopped, or diced. (A simple rule of thumb is that the smaller the cut, the more intense the flavor. Feel free to adjust the size of the cut in the following recipes in order to increase or decrease the included garlic's pungency.) In order to bring out the full flavor of the garlic, sauté it over medium-low heat, stirring often with a wooden spoon. Do not allow the garlic to cook too fast or to become overly brown, or it will taste bitter. When it reaches a pale golden color, that is the time to add other ingredients or remove it from the heat.

If you like just a hint of garlic, place a couple of cut cloves into a sauce while it simmers; remove with a slotted spoon before serving. The flavor will be very subtle.

To remove the smell of garlic from your hands, rinse your hands in cool water and rub them with the cut side of a lemon or with a teaspoon of table salt. Within 15 seconds, the smell will be gone.

Vampire Quotient

As hard as it is to believe, not everyone loves garlic. Some people, in fact, fear and despise it. Let's just say that they don't know what they're missing. That being said, most of the recipes in this cookbook can be modified for the vampires among you by reducing the garlic it or omitting it altogether. They'll still taste good . . . but perhaps just not as fantastic as they are *with* the garlic.

If your dining companion is a vampire, but you simply can't help yourself from indulging, try chewing on a sprig of parsley after the meal to erase the traces of garlic on your breath. Crunching on an espresso bean works too; fresh mint is another way to eliminate stinky breath. Did someone say *mojito*?

A DRINK WHILE YOU DECIDE WHAT TO EAT?

*Before you head to the store,
mix up one of these cocktails, which are guaranteed
to bring out your sense of adventure!*

THE STINKING BLOODY MARY 👉

Some people will tell you that the Bloody Mary was named for Mary Tudor, daughter of Henry VIII, who earned her grisly moniker by killing off her adversaries. Others say that Mary was the girlfriend of a bartender who invented the drink. Whoever the real Mary was, we think that her namesake drink is greatly improved with a bit of garlic. Serve this with Sunday brunch, and things are sure to get lively!

Ice cubes, for chilling and shaking

1 cup tomato juice

3 ounces vodka

1 teaspoon prepared horseradish

1 teaspoon Worcestershire sauce

½ teaspoon Tabasco sauce

½ teaspoon minced garlic

Splash of olive juice

½ teaspoon freshly ground black pepper

Juice of 1 lemon

Celery spears (optional), pickled garlic cloves, large cocktail olives, and cherry tomatoes, for garnish

1 Chill 2 pint glasses in the freezer beforehand, or fill them with ice cubes and water and let stand for 1 minute before using. Fill a cocktail shaker with ice and add the tomato juice, vodka, horseradish, Worcestershire sauce, Tabasco sauce, minced garlic, olive juice, pepper, and lemon juice. Shake vigorously for 15 to 30 seconds. Divide between the 2 chilled glasses and garnish with a celery spear and a skewer with a pickled garlic clove, cocktail olive, and cherry tomato.

Serves 2

THE INFAMOUS GARTINI 👉

This drink is for the reckless, fearless thrill seeker. It says "I'm going to have garlic breath, and the devil may care!" In order to make it, you'll need to find a jar of garlic-stuffed olives, which can be found in the gourmet section of your local market. Bottoms up!

> Ice cubes, for chilling and shaking
> 4 garlic-stuffed olives or pickled garlic cloves
> 4 ounces vodka
> Dash of dry vermouth
> Splash of olive juice (optional)

1 Chill 2 martini glasses in the freezer beforehand, or fill them with ice cubes and water and let stand for 1 minute before using. Spear the olives on a cocktail pick, using 2 olives on each pick.

2 Fill a cocktail shaker with ice and add the vodka and vermouth. For a "dirty" martini, add a splash of the olive juice from the jar. Shake vigorously for 15 seconds. Strain into the 2 chilled glasses and garnish with the garlic-stuffed olives.

Serves 2

TO BEGIN YOUR MEAL

Appetizers are delicious small bites designed to whet the appetite. Here, we've collected an assortment of our most-requested starters.

BAGNA CALDA

*I**f you were a clove of garlic, this is where you'd want to be . . . lounging in a warm bath of olive oil, with lots of other cloves for company and the occasional anchovy for amusement. At the restaurant, we serve this with warm focaccia buns; at home, use your favorite bread to sop up this fragrant concoction.*

> 2½ cups garlic cloves, skins intact
> 2 cups olive oil
> ¼ cup unsalted butter, cut into bits
> 1 (2-ounce) can anchovies

1 Preheat the oven to 275°F. Put the garlic cloves into a heavy glass or ceramic baking dish and pour the olive oil over the top. Sprinkle the butter over the garlic. Lay the anchovies in a single layer on top.

2 Cover with aluminum foil and bake for 1½ hours, or until the garlic cloves are dense and limp. Remove one clove to test; let it cool for a moment, then squeeze it gently between your fingers. The garlic should immediately burst onto your fingers, indicating that it is soft and spreadable.

3 Remove from the oven. Serve with bread or other dippers.

Serves 4 to 6

TOASTED BREAD & MOZZARELLA SPIEDINI

*T*he Italian word spiedini *refers to a skewer laced with bite-sized pieces of meat or fish or otherwise and cooked under a broiler. In our version, we've taken wooden skewers and threaded them with cubes of mozzarella cheese and bread. When unexpected guests drop by, whip up a batch of these and shake up a few Gartinis (page 5), and you've got a party!*

 1 sourdough or sweet baguette
 1 clove garlic, halved, plus 1 clove garlic, minced
 12 ounces mozzarella cheese, cut into
  1-inch cubes
 3 tablespoons olive oil
 Juice of 1 lemon

1 Preheat the oven to 350°F. With a serrated bread knife, cut the baguette into 1-inch cubes. Rub one or two sides of each cube with the cut edge of the garlic halves.

2 On a wooden skewer, alternate cubes of bread with cubes of cheese, leaving ½ inch on either side of the skewer for easy handling. Place the skewers on a baking sheet. In a small bowl, combine the olive oil, lemon juice, and minced garlic. Using a pastry brush, lightly brush the mixture over the top of the skewers and let them stand for about 10 minutes.

3 Bake for 4 to 5 minutes, until the bread cubes are golden brown and the cheese is beginning to soften around the edges.

4 Serve immediately.

Makes 10 to 12 skewers

FRIED CASTROVILLE ARTICHOKE HEARTS

astroville, California, is the self-proclaimed "Artichoke Capitol of the World," with the perfect climate for growing artichokes. Citizens of Castroville hold a festival every year with artichokes galore; this is our garlicky version of one of the dishes sold there.

8 to 10 medium artichokes, or 2 (10-ounce) cans whole artichoke hearts in water, drained and patted dry

1 teaspoon freshly squeezed lemon juice

1 large egg

1 teaspoon salt

1 teaspoon freshly ground black pepper

½ cup all-purpose flour

1 cup finely ground polenta

1 teaspoon ground cumin

1 teaspoon chili powder

1 teaspoon sweet paprika

1 tablespoon garlic salt

Vegetable oil, for deep-frying

2 lemons, cut into wedges

Roasted Garlic and Basil Aioli (page 159)

1 To prepare the fresh artichokes, peel away the tough outer layer of leaves and trim the stem to about 1 inch. Chop off the tops of the remaining leaves with a sharp knife, leaving about 1 inch of leaves pro-truding from the stem. Using a paring knife, peel away the remaining

ring of layers that surround the heart. Scrape out the fuzzy choke with a spoon. Trim the top of the heart with a paring knife so that it's clean and smooth. Place the hearts into a shallow bowl of ice water and gently stir in the lemon juice (the lemon juice will keep the artichokes from turning brown).

2 In a small bowl, beat the egg, salt, and pepper together; pour into a heavy, resealable plastic bag. In a separate bowl, combine the flour, polenta, cumin, chili powder, paprika, and garlic salt. Stir to blend.

3 Working with 2 to 3 artichoke hearts at a time, toss the artichokes in the bag and shake to coat with the egg mixture. Remove from the bag and dredge in the flour mixture, tossing with a fork to coat them evenly. Tap off the excess flour and place the hearts on a plate.

4 In a large, heavy skillet, heat 1 to 2 inches of oil over high heat to 375°F; it should be hot and bubbly.

5 Working in small batches, carefully lower the artichoke hearts into the oil and fry until golden brown and crisp, about 3 minutes. Using a slotted spoon, transfer them to paper towels to drain.

6 Transfer the hearts to a serving platter and place the lemon wedges around the edges. Serve with the aioli for dipping.

Serves 4 to 6

ITALIAN POT STICKERS

North Beach, the Italian district of San Francisco where the original Stinking Rose Restaurant is located, is just around the corner from Chinatown. Both neighborhoods are noisy and colorful, inspiring food combinations such as this Italian version of Chinese pot stickers. Stuffed with spicy sausage and mushrooms, and served with a tangy dipping sauce, they make a delightful dinner starter or tasty summer lunch.

FILLING

2 tablespoons sesame oil

1 pound ground pork or Italian sausage meat, removed from casings

½ cup finely chopped celery

2 tablespoons minced fresh ginger

10 to 12 cloves garlic, minced

½ pound white or cremini mushrooms, finely chopped

½ cup finely chopped red bell pepper

¼ cup rice wine vinegar

¼ cup soy sauce

Salt and freshly ground black pepper

1 bunch cilantro, stemmed and chopped

1 bunch green onions, including green parts, chopped

12 to 15 pot sticker or wonton wrappers

 CONTINUED

GINGER-SOY DIPPING SAUCE

1 cup rice wine vinegar

½ cup water

¼ cup sugar

1 tablespoon minced fresh ginger

2 cloves garlic, sliced

½ teaspoon red pepper flakes

¼ cup sesame oil

1¼ cups light soy sauce

2 cups loosely packed mixed salad greens

1 tablespoon extra-virgin olive oil

4 to 5 cherry tomatoes, halved

2 teaspoons black sesame seeds

1 To make the filling: In a heavy skillet, heat the sesame oil over medium heat. Add the pork, celery, ginger, and garlic and cook, stirring occasionally, for 5 to 7 minutes, until the pork is browned and the celery is crisp-tender. Remove the skillet from the heat and drain off the fat, then add the mushrooms and return to medium heat for 5 minutes, stirring occasionally. Stir in the bell pepper, vinegar, and soy sauce and season with salt and pepper. Cook for 3 minutes, stirring frequently. Stir in the cilantro and green onions, then remove from the heat and let cool to room temperature.

2 On a work surface, lay the wrappers flat and place 1 tablespoon filling in the center of each wrapper. Fold each wrapper in half, sealing the edges with the tines of a fork. Dip a pastry brush in cold water and brush lightly over the top of each pot sticker. Arrange in a single layer on a small baking sheet and refrigerate for about 20 minutes to chill.

3 To make the dipping sauce: In a small saucepan, combine the vinegar, water, sugar, ginger, garlic, and pepper flakes. Bring to a boil over medium heat, then decrease the heat to low and simmer for 15 minutes. Remove from the heat and add the sesame oil and soy sauce. Strain through a sieve lined with cheesecloth into a small bowl and refrigerate for at least 10 minutes.

4 Pour about ½ cup water into a heavy, nonstick sauté pan and put the pot stickers in the pan. The water level should be at about one-fourth the height of the pot stickers. Cover the pan and place over medium heat. Bring the water to a rolling boil and cook for 3 minutes, or until the pot stickers are browned on the bottom and shiny on top. The water will evaporate during cooking, so watch carefully so that the pot stickers don't burn. Remove from the heat.

5 To serve, arrange the salad greens on a serving dish, drizzle the olive oil over the top, gently toss, then arrange the pot stickers on top. Drizzle 2 tablespoons of the dipping sauce over the pot stickers and greens. Sprinkle with the tomatoes and sesame seeds. Serve immediately with the remaining dipping sauce alongside.

Serves 4 to 6

POPCORN CALAMARI

 hese crisp, bite-sized calamari are so tasty and fun to eat—they're like popcorn for grown-ups! We recommend serving them with a ramekin of the cocktail sauce in this recipe or with Roasted Garlic and Basil Aioli (page 159).

COCKTAIL SAUCE

½ cup ketchup

2 teaspoons prepared horseradish

1 tablespoon freshly squeezed orange juice

1 teaspoon minced fresh ginger

2 pounds fresh or thawed frozen small calamari

1 large egg

1 teaspoon salt

1 teaspoon freshly ground black pepper

½ cup all-purpose flour

1 cup finely ground polenta

1 teaspoon ground cumin

1 teaspoon chili powder

1 teaspoon sweet paprika

1 tablespoon garlic salt

Vegetable oil, for deep-frying

2 lemons, cut into wedges

1 To make the cocktail sauce: Combine all the ingredients in a small bowl and stir well. Transfer to a small ramekin. Cover and refrigerate.

2 If the calamari are not already cleaned, cut off the tentacles just above the eyes; reserve the tentacles. Squeeze the round beak from the end of the tentacles. Hold the tail end of each body on a cutting board with one hand and scrape the side of a large knife along the body, pressing hard, to remove the innards. Holding the tail end, pull out the long quill. Rinse the bodies well inside and out under cold running water. Cut the bodies and tentacles into ½-inch-thick rings. Pat dry with a paper towel.

3 In a small bowl, beat the egg with the salt and pepper; pour into a heavy resealable plastic bag. In a separate bowl, combine the flour, polenta, cumin, chili powder, paprika, and garlic salt. Stir to blend.

4 Put 5 to 7 calamari pieces in the bag and seal; shake the bag to coat the rings evenly. Open the bag and remove the calamari. Dredge them in the flour mixture, tossing with a fork, until coated entirely. Tap off the excess flour and place on a plate. Repeat to coat the remaining calamari pieces.

5 In a large, heavy skillet, heat 1 to 2 inches of oil over high heat to 375°F; it should be hot and bubbly.

6 Working in small batches, carefully lower the calamari into the oil and fry until golden brown and crisp, about 3 minutes. Using a slotted spoon, transfer to paper towels to drain. Transfer to a serving platter and place the lemon wedges around the edges. Serve with the cocktail sauce alongside.

Serves 4 to 8

CREAMY GARLIC-SPINACH CHEESE FONDUE

Garlic has numerous documented health benefits, from lowering cholesterol to boosting the immune system. It is said to be good for expectant mothers, preventing complications during pregnancy and delivery. Whether or not you're eating garlic for your health, this recipe makes it fun to get your garlic—who doesn't love ooey-gooey melted cheese? Once you dip in, we dare you to stop!

2 tablespoons unsalted butter

3 cloves garlic, diced

⅔ cup dry white wine

4 cups (1 pound) shredded Fontina cheese

1½ cups (6 ounces) shredded Gruyère cheese

2 teaspoons cornstarch

2 cups finely chopped spinach leaves

¼ cup heavy cream

Salt and freshly ground black pepper

1 tablespoon minced fresh chives

OPTIONAL DIPPERS

Chilled cooked shrimp

Steamed asparagus spears

Zucchini, cut into matchsticks

White mushrooms

☞ CONTINUED

Cherry tomatoes

Stuffed or shaped pasta (such as rigatoni or ravioli), cooked
al dente

Bread cubes (such as sourdough, walnut, or a buttery croissant)

Crackers or bread sticks

1 In a heavy saucepan, melt the butter over medium-low heat. Add the garlic and sauté for 2 to 3 minutes, until it becomes golden brown around the edges. Be careful not to overcook the garlic, or it will become bitter. Add the wine. In a bowl, toss the cheeses with the cornstarch to coat. Add the cheeses to the pan, 1 cup at a time, stirring frequently until the cheese melts before adding the next cup. Add the spinach and the cream. Stir until the mixture becomes creamy and smooth. Season with salt and pepper.

2 Transfer the mixture to a fondue pot over low heat, or pour into a warmed ceramic ramekin. Sprinkle with the minced chives. Serve immediately, with your choice of dippers.

Serves 2 to 4

TUSCAN WHITE BEAN SOUP WITH PESTO 👉

We discovered an old book on natural remedies that prescribes garlic as a cure for flatulence. Does that mean that garlic and beans are the absolutely perfect combination? We'll let you do your own research on that. You might start with this soup.

2 cups dried cannellini beans, or 2 (10-ounce) cans great Northern or other white beans, drained and rinsed

5 to 7 cloves roasted garlic (*page 155*)

3 tablespoons olive oil

1 yellow onion, diced

1 (14.5-ounce) can chopped tomatoes with juice

1 tablespoon minced fresh rosemary

1 tablespoon minced fresh thyme

Salt and freshly ground black pepper

4 to 6 tablespoons Basil Pesto, for drizzling (*recipe follows*)

1 If using dried beans, rinse and pick over them. Put the beans in large pot, add cold water to cover the beans by 3 to 4 inches, and soak overnight.

2 Thoroughly drain the beans and return to the pot. Cover with water by 2 to 3 inches and bring to a boil over medium heat. Decrease the heat to low and simmer, stirring occasionally, for about 1½ hours, or until the beans are soft enough to mash easily with the back of a spoon. Remove from the heat.

3 Transfer three-fourths of the beans to a blender and ladle in a generous spoonful of the cooking liquid. Add the roasted garlic. Pulse on high speed until the beans are blended but still chunky, adding more cooking liquid if needed. Drain the remaining beans and set aside, reserving 1 cup of the cooking liquid.

4 In a heavy saucepan, heat the olive oil over medium heat and sauté the onion until golden brown, about 5 minutes. Stir in the tomatoes, rosemary, and thyme and season with salt and pepper. Decrease the heat and simmer for 5 minutes. Add the reserved whole beans and simmer for another 5 minutes. Add the blended beans and stir to combine thoroughly. If the soup seems too thick, add a few tablespoons of the reserved cooking liquid. Simmer for 10 to 15 minutes to combine the flavors.

5 Ladle the soup into warmed shallow soup bowls and drizzle a generous tablespoon of pesto over each. Serve immediately.

Serves 4 to 6

BASIL PESTO

3 cloves garlic, coarsely chopped

½ cup pine nuts

½ cup (2 ounces) grated Parmesan cheese

2 cups loosely packed fresh basil leaves

½ cup best-quality extra-virgin olive oil

1 teaspoon salt

½ teaspoon freshly ground black pepper

1 In a blender or food processor, combine the garlic, pine nuts, cheese, and basil. Pulse on low speed until the mixture is finely chopped. With the machine running, gradually drizzle in the olive oil until thoroughly incorporated. Add the salt and pepper and process a bit longer. Use now, or store in the refrigerator for up to 1 week.

Makes 1½ cups

NOTE

Pesto should be stored in a glass or earthenware container; avoid using metal or plastic containers. If you want to store pesto for longer than one week, don't add the garlic or cheese until just before you're ready to use it. To prevent discoloration and oxidation, cover the top of the pesto with a thin film of olive oil.

GARLIC HUMMUS

 ges and ages ago, the cradles of newborns were festooned with garlic bulbs to ward off fairies who might take a liking to a sweet-faced babe and carry it away into the netherworld. While you might not have to go to such lengths to keep your own offspring safe, you might want to mix up a batch of this for them to snack on after school. Or, just make it for yourself, because you very much deserve it.

1 (10-ounce) can garbanzo beans, drained and rinsed
¼ cup extra virgin olive oil
Juice of ½ lemon
4 cloves roasted garlic *(page 155)*
Salt and freshly ground black pepper
1 tablespoon minced fresh flat-leaf parsley
Toasted artisan bread or crackers, for serving

1 In a blender, combine the beans, olive oil, lemon juice, and roasted garlic. Process on low speed until smooth and creamy. Season with salt and pepper. Use now, or cover and refrigerate for up to 1 week.

2 To serve, scrape into a serving dish. Sprinkle the parsley over the hummus and serve with toast or crackers for spreading or dipping.

Serves 4 to 6

NOTE

The thick, creamy texture and roasted garlic flavor of this spread also make it a lovely dipping sauce for roasted meats.

POTATO-ONION SOUP EN CROUTE

ount Dracula might have served a soup like this at a dinner party at his mansion—sans the garlic, of course. This rich, creamy concoction is made with potatoes and chicken broth, ladled into individual terrines and covered with a buttery, flaky crust. Ooh, la la.

2 tablespoons olive oil

2 cups diced white or yellow onions

10 garlic cloves, thinly sliced

4 cups chicken broth

1 pound russet or Yukon Gold potatoes, peeled and diced (about 2 cups)

½ cup heavy cream

Salt and freshly ground black pepper

1 package thawed frozen puff pastry

1 tablespoon unsalted butter, melted

1 Preheat the oven to 350°F. Heat the olive oil in a large skillet with a tight-fitting lid over medium-low heat. Add the onions and sauté, stirring frequently, for about 5 minutes, or until translucent. Add the garlic and sauté for 2 to 3 more minutes, until the garlic becomes translucent around the edges and the onions are golden brown. Gradually pour in the chicken broth, 1 cup at a time, stirring gently to incorporate. Add the potatoes, increase the heat to high, and bring the mixture to a boil. When

 CONTINUED

large bubbles appear on the surface, decrease the heat to low and cover. Simmer for 30 to 40 minutes, until the potatoes become soft and are easily mashed with the back of a wooden spoon. Remove from the heat. Cool for about 5 minutes, then pour into a blender and blend on medium speed until thick and creamy. Pour the mixture back into the pan and slowly add the cream, stirring to combine thoroughly; the soup should be thick and velvety. Season with salt and pepper.

2 Arrange four 4-inch ceramic soup terrines or ramekins in a row and divide the soup among them. Cut four 5-inch squares from the defrosted puff pastry. With a pastry brush, apply some of the melted butter to the rim of each of the terrines. Place a puff pastry square over the top of each terrine, pressing the dough around the edges with your fingertips to seal the dough around the sides of the dish. Brush melted butter over the top of the pastry crust and puncture the crust with a fork two or three times.

3 Place the terrines on a baking sheet and bake for 12 minutes, or until the dough puffs up and turns a light golden brown. Remove from the oven and serve hot.

Serves 4

THE STINKING ROSE HOUSE SALAD

Most house salads are just boring piles of lettuce on a plate. Not so with our house salad! We are the Empire of Stink, after all, and we can't let our fans down with a salad that fails to titillate the taste buds. Our house greens are bursting with green, garlicky crunch. Serve this, and we promise that no one at your table will be tempted to yawn.

DRESSING

2 cloves roasted garlic (*page 155*)

2 cloves garlic, minced

1 teaspoon minced fresh ginger

2 tablespoons freshly squeezed orange juice

Juice of 1 lemon

⅓ cup extra-virgin olive oil

3 thick slices day-old bread (preferably sourdough), crusts on and cubed

2 tablespoons olive oil

5 cups mixed salad greens

Salt and freshly ground black pepper

1 cup cherry tomatoes, halved

1 To make the dressing: In a small bowl, mash the roasted garlic cloves with the back of a spoon until they form a paste. Add the minced garlic, ginger, orange juice, and lemon juice and whisk until combined. Gradually add the ⅓ cup olive oil, whisking until the dressing is opaque and creamy.

2 Adjust an oven rack to the middle position and preheat the broiler. Toss the bread cubes in a bowl with the 2 tablespoons olive oil. Spread the bread cubes on a baking sheet and toast under the broiler for about 1 minute. Remove the pan and shake the cubes, then place under the broiler again for about 1 minute, or until golden brown and crunchy. Remove from the broiler.

3 Put the salad greens in a salad bowl and toss with the dressing. Season with salt and pepper, add the tomatoes and croutons, and toss again. Serve immediately.

Serves 4

GARLICKY CAESAR SALAD 👉

*I*n honor of the notorious Roman ruler, we packed this classic salad with crunchy romaine, freshly cut croutons, and a dressing laced with anchovies and garlic. If Caesar had been lucky enough to get a taste of this, he surely would have asked for seconds! It can easily be turned into a full lunch by topping it with slices of grilled chicken breast or salmon.

DRESSING

4 anchovy fillets

2 large egg yolks, or 4 tablespoons pasteurized egg yolk mix

1 teaspoon Dijon mustard

Juice of ½ lemon

½ cup extra-virgin olive oil

3 thick slices day-old bread (preferably sourdough), crusts on and cubed

2 tablespoons olive oil

2 large cloves garlic, halved

1 pound (16 to 20 leaves) hearts of romaine lettuce

¼ cup (1 ounce) shaved best-quality Parmesan cheese

Freshly cracked black pepper

1 To make the dressing: In a small bowl, mash the anchovy fillets with the back of a wooden spoon until they are pulverized. With a fork, mix in the egg yolks. Add the mustard, lemon juice, and olive oil, whisking vigorously to combine.

2 Adjust an oven rack to the middle position and preheat the broiler. Toss the bread cubes in a bowl with the 2 tablespoons olive oil. Spread the bread cubes on a baking sheet and toast under the broiler for about 1 minute. Remove the pan and shake the cubes, then place under the broiler again for 1 minute, or until golden brown and crunchy. Remove from the broiler.

3 Rub the cut edges of the garlic cloves over the interior of a salad bowl. Put the lettuce leaves in the bowl, pour the dressing over the top, and toss with your hands to gently coat each leaf.

4 Divide among salad plates and sprinkle with the shaved cheese and pepper. Scatter the croutons over the tops. Serve immediately.

Serves 4

ARUGULA SALAD WITH ROASTED TOMATOES & MAUI ONIONS 👉

hen your mama told you to eat your greens, she must have known how good they are for you. Which means that the combination of greens and garlic is really something special! Garlic is a known insect repellent—its aromatic qualities apparently make the blood quite unappetizing for mosquitoes and other creepy-crawlies. With that in mind, this salad is a perfect choice for alfresco dining on a warm summer's night. If you can't find Maui onions at your local grocer, ask for another type of sweet onion, such as Vidalia or Walla Walla.

1 cup oven-roasted tomatoes (*page 158*)

1 (10-ounce) can garbanzo beans, drained and rinsed

1 Maui onion or other sweet onion, sliced into very thin rings

2½ cups loosely packed baby arugula

2 tablespoons extra-virgin olive oil

Juice of ½ lemon

Sea salt and freshly ground black pepper

¼ cup garlic chips (*page 152*)

1 In a deep bowl, combine the tomatoes, beans, and onion slices. Add the arugula and toss lightly. Drizzle with the olive oil and lemon juice and toss again. Season with salt and pepper.

2 To serve, divide among salad plates and sprinkle with the garlic chips.

Serves 4

BASIL PESTO, MOZZARELLA & TOMATO PIZZETTES ☞

his is our version of the most traditional of Italian pizzas, the Margherita—only instead of basil leaves, we use a basil pesto. The result is rich, yet satisfyingly simple.

½ recipe pizza dough *(page 162)*
½ cup Basil Pesto *(page 25)*
Cornmeal, for sprinkling
¼ cup (1 ounce) shredded mozzarella cheese
¼ cup cherry tomatoes in various colors, halved

1 Preheat the oven to 425°F. With floured hands, stretch each ball of dough into a rough oval about 8 inches long and 4 inches wide.

2 Flour the surface of a lightly greased baking sheet and sprinkle with cornmeal. Place the 2 dough ovals on the pan. Spread ¼ cup pesto over each pizza to generously coat the dough, leaving a ½-inch border around the edges. Sprinkle each crust with half of the cheese and tomatoes. Bake for 7 to 10 minutes, until the edges of the crust are golden and the cheese is bubbly. Remove from the oven and serve immediately.

Makes 2 pizzettes

ARUGULA, CHERRY TOMATO, BASIL & SMOKED MOZZARELLA PIZZETTES

his pizza is like a party in your mouth! With a cast of roasted garlic cloves, smoked mozzarella cheese, colorful tomatoes and peppery arugula, this combination of flavors and textures is a perfect kick-start to any meal. Just don't blame us if you feel like standing up and dancing around the table.

½ recipe pizza dough *(page 162)*

Cornmeal, for sprinkling

4 tablespoons extra-virgin olive oil

Salt and freshly ground black pepper

8 leaves fresh basil

¼ cup cherry tomatoes in various colors, halved

¼ cup (1 ounce) shredded smoked mozzarella cheese

2 cloves roasted garlic *(page 155)*

½ teaspoon minced fresh ginger

1 tablespoon freshly squeezed orange juice

Juice of ½ lemon

½ cup firmly packed baby arugula

1 Preheat the oven to 425°F. With floured hands, stretch each ball of dough into a rough oval about 8 inches long and 4 inches wide.

 CONTINUED

2 Flour the surface of a lightly greased baking sheet and sprinkle with cornmeal. Place the 2 dough ovals on the pan. Spread 1 tablespoon of the olive oil over each crust with a pastry brush; sprinkle with salt and pepper. Scatter 4 basil leaves and half of the tomatoes over each crust and sprinkle each with half of the cheese. Bake for 7 to 10 minutes, until the edges of the crust are golden and the cheese is bubbly.

3 While the pizzettes are baking, put the roasted garlic cloves in a bowl and mash them with the back of a spoon until they form a paste. Add the ginger, orange juice, and lemon juice and whisk until combined. Gradually add the remaining 2 tablespoons olive oil, whisking until the dressing is opaque and creamy. Add the arugula and toss to completely coat the leaves.

4 Remove the pizzettes from the oven and mound the arugula on top. Serve immediately.

Makes 2 pizzettes

KALAMATA OLIVE, ROASTED GARLIC & SMOKED MOZZARELLA PIZZETTES

his pie has some zing! The olives add a vinegary kick to balance the roasted sweetness of the garlic, and the combination is so tasty that we doubt there will be any left over for breakfast.

2 anchovy fillets

I large egg yolk, or 2 tablespoons pasteurized egg yolk mix

I large clove garlic, diced

½ teaspoon Dijon mustard

Juice of ½ lemon

¼ cup plus 2 tablespoons olive oil

Freshly ground black pepper

¼ cup kalamata olives, pitted

½ recipe pizza dough *(page 162)*

Cornmeal, for sprinkling

¼ cup roasted garlic cloves *(page 155)*

¼ cup (I ounce) shredded smoked mozzarella cheese

1 Preheat the oven to 425°F. In a bowl, mash the anchovy fillets with the back of wooden spoon until they are pulverized. With a fork, mix in the egg yolk. Add the garlic, mustard, lemon juice, and the ¼ cup olive oil and whisk vigorously to combine. Season with pepper, add the olives, and toss to coat thoroughly. Let stand for 5 minutes.

 CONTINUED

2 With floured hands, stretch each ball of dough into a rough oval about 8 inches long and 4 inches wide.

3 Flour the surface of a lightly greased baking sheet and sprinkle with cornmeal. Place the 2 dough ovals on the pan. Spread 1 tablespoon olive oil over each crust with a pastry brush. Spoon half of the olives with the dressing over the top of each crust and sprinkle each with half of the roasted garlic and cheese.

4 Bake for 8 to 12 minutes, until the edges of the crust are golden and the cheese is bubbly. Remove from the oven and serve immediately.

Makes 2 pizzettes

BBQ CHICKEN, CILANTRO & MOZZARELLA PIZZETTES

ot surprisingly, Rose Pizzettes are not the normal pizza pies that you find else-
where. We make our own dough and stretch it into an oval shape, then pile the
thin crust with all kinds of yummy toppings.

½ recipe pizza dough *(page 162)*

Cornmeal, for sprinkling

¼ cup Barbecue Sauce *(recipe follows)*

½ cup shredded cooked chicken breast

2 tablespoons chopped fresh cilantro

½ small red onion, sliced into thin rings

¼ cup (1 ounce) shredded mozzarella cheese

Cilantro sprigs, for garnish

1 Preheat the oven to 425°F. With floured hands, stretch each ball of
dough into a rough oval about 8 inches long and 4 inches wide.

2 Flour the surface of a lightly greased baking sheet and sprinkle with
cornmeal. Place the 2 dough ovals on the pan. Spread half of the sauce
over each dough oval, leaving a ½-inch border. Sprinkle each crust with
half of the chicken, cilantro, and red onion rings and top each with half
of the cheese.

CONTINUED

3 Bake for 8 to 12 minutes, until the edges of the crust are golden and the cheese is bubbly. Remove from the oven and garnish with sprigs of cilantro. Serve immediately.

Makes 2 pizzettes

BARBECUE SAUCE

½ cup ketchup

¼ cup apple cider vinegar

¼ cup firmly packed brown sugar

½ teaspoon ground cinnamon

2 tablespoons soy sauce

I tablespoon Dijon mustard

I tablespoon chili powder

I teaspoon grated fresh ginger

I tablespoon freshly squeezed lemon juice

2 tablespoons Worcestershire sauce

2 cloves roasted garlic (*page 155*), mashed into a paste

1 In a small saucepan, combine all the ingredients. Place over medium heat and simmer for 15 minutes, stirring frequently, to combine the flavors. Remove from the heat and let cool.

2 Use now, or refrigerate in an airtight container for up to 2 weeks.

Makes 1 cup

SHIITAKE MUSHROOM, ASPARAGUS & MOZZARELLA PIZZA FINGERS

We've combined the smoky tang of shitake mushrooms with spears of asparagus and mozzarella cheese for a pizza that is full of grown-up flavor. But that doesn't mean that you can't have fun while you're eating it. Who needs silverware? Just pick up the pieces and enjoy.

½ recipe pizza dough (*page 162*)

Cornmeal, for sprinkling

2 tablespoons extra-virgin olive oil

Salt and freshly ground black pepper

3 ounces shiitake mushrooms, stemmed and sliced (about ½ cup)

14 to 16 cloves roasted garlic (*page 155*)

8 spears asparagus

¼ cup (1 ounce) shredded mozzarella cheese

1 tablespoon minced fresh flat-leaf parsley

1 Preheat the oven to 425°F. With floured hands, stretch each ball of dough into a rough oval about 8 inches long and 4 inches wide.

2 Flour the surface of a lightly greased baking sheet and sprinkle with cornmeal. Place the 2 dough ovals on the pan. Spread 1 tablespoon of the olive oil over each crust with a pastry brush; sprinkle with salt and pepper. Scatter half of the mushrooms and roasted garlic over the top

 CONTINUED

of each crust. Lay 4 asparagus spears lengthwise on each pizza and sprinkle each with half of the cheese and parsley.

3 Bake for 8 to 12 minutes, until the edges of the crust are golden and the cheese is bubbly. Remove from the oven and slice between the asparagus spears to make long pizza "fingers." Serve immediately.

Makes 8 pizza fingers

SKILLET-ROASTED MUSSELS WITH GARLIC DIPPING BUTTER

Chef Andrea Froncillo created this recipe while daydreaming of his boyhood days spent near the seaside in Napoli. His method wasn't sophisticated back then—roasting the mussels on the beach with a splash of seawater was as fancy as he got—but now this sizzling skillet is a Stinking Rose signature. When we hear gasps of "ooh" and "ahh" from the dining room, it's usually because a sizzling skillet has just been delivered to a table. We start with a cast-iron skillet and load it up with mussels. As soon as it's delivered to the table, we drizzle it with a "sizzle sauce," which creates a dramatic and fragrant steam. Mmm . . .

1 pound Prince Edward Island mussels, debearded and scrubbed

Garlic salt

Freshly ground black pepper

Leaves from 2 sprigs flat-leaf parsley, minced

2 tablespoons soy sauce

2 tablespoons dry white wine

Garlic Compound Butter (page 154), for serving

1 Heat a large cast-iron skillet over high heat for about 2 minutes, or until the surface is hot enough that water bounces and sizzles when sprinkled in it. Add the mussels to the hot skillet and cook for 4 to 5 minutes,

 CONTINUED

until the shells begin to open. Remove from the heat and discard any mussels that don't open. Sprinkle generously with the garlic salt and pepper, then the parsley.

2 In a cup, combine the soy sauce and wine. Bring the hot skillet directly to the table, placing it on a heavy trivet. Pour the soy mixture over the mussels; it will sizzle and steam, a lovely effect. Place the ramekin of compound butter in the center of the skillet. Pry each mussel out of its shell with a seafood fork, dunk into the butter, and eat immediately!

Serves 4

SKILLET-ROASTED SHRIMP

t turns out that mussels aren't the only sea creature that tastes good when roasted in an iron skillet; shrimp, too, are finger-licking good when roasted in the shell, and then peeled and eaten at the table. Just don't forget the warm hand towels!

3 tablespoons olive oil

1 teaspoon grated lemon zest

4 teaspoons minced fresh flat-leaf parsley

1 teaspoon garlic salt

1½ pounds large shrimp (21 to 30 per pound) in the shell

Freshly ground black pepper

Garlic Compound Butter (*page 154*), for serving

1 In a bowl, combine the olive oil, lemon zest, 2 teaspoons of the parsley, and the garlic salt. Add the shrimp and toss to coat. Refrigerate for 30 minutes to 1 hour.

2 Heat a large cast-iron skillet over high heat for about 2 minutes, or until the surface is hot enough that water bounces and sizzles when sprinkled in it. Arrange the shrimp in a single layer in the hot skillet and cook for 3 to 4 minutes on each side, or until the shrimp become a rosy pink color. Remove from the heat. Sprinkle with the pepper and the remaining 2 teaspoons parsley.

3 Bring the hot skillet directly to the table, placing it on a heavy trivet. Place the ramekin of compound butter in the center of the skillet. With your fingers, peel each shrimp and dunk it into the compound butter.

Serves 4 to 6

PASTA DISHES

*Noodles, noodles, and more noodles . . .
who doesn't love pasta? We've collected the best pasta
dishes from our menus to share with you. Just remember
the meaning of al dente (no, he isn't a cousin of Al Capone):
the literal Italian translation is "to the tooth," and it
means that properly cooked pasta should be firm when
bitten, yet cooked all the way through. Unless otherwise
indicated, all recipes below are for entrée-size portions.*

CAPELLINI WITH CHERRY TOMATOES, OLIVES & BASIL ☞

id you know that the Soviet Army distributed so much garlic among its troops during World Wars I and II that the soldiers nicknamed it "Russian penicillin"? If you're in need of an immune boost, this recipe is one delicious way to get it. This colorful dish can be prepared in less than 15 minutes for a quick lunch or a first course. The quality of the pasta here is of paramount importance; we suggest that you buy fresh pasta, which tends to be silkier and more aromatic than dried, for the best, most flavorful results. Fresh pasta is available in gourmet markets as well as in the refrigerated section of most supermarkets.

16 ounces fresh capellini pasta, or 12 ounces dried

2 tablespoons olive oil

8 to 10 cloves roasted garlic *(page 155)*

1 pint cherry tomatoes in various colors, halved

½ cup kalamata olives, pitted and coarsely chopped

1 teaspoon red pepper flakes

Salt and freshly ground black pepper

6 to 8 leaves fresh basil, coarsely chopped

1 In a large pot of salted boiling water, cook the fresh pasta for 1 to 2 minutes, until al dente. If using dried pasta, cook according to the package directions, until al dente. Drain well.

2 In a large cast-iron skillet, heat the olive oil over medium heat and add the garlic, tomatoes, olives, and red pepper flakes. Stir once or twice to heat the ingredients through, then add the pasta, tossing to coat completely. Season with salt and pepper. Remove from the heat. Scoop the pasta into a serving bowl and sprinkle with the basil. Serve immediately.

Serves 4 as a first course or light lunch

PASTA WITH BUTTERNUT SQUASH, FRIED SAGE & GARLIC CHIPS ☞

*S*ince garlic contains only 4 calories per clove, it is definitely the most guilt-free way to add flavor that we've ever found! In this dish, we've combined the sweet flavor of oven-roasted butternut squash with butter-crisped sage and accented it with the crunch of garlic chips. Go ahead—have another helping!

1 (1-pound) butternut squash, halved and seeded

1 tablespoon olive oil

Salt and freshly ground black pepper

2 tablespoons unsalted butter

1 bunch sage, stemmed

1 pound gemelli pasta

Garlic chips (*page 152*)

1 Preheat the oven to 400°F. Peel the squash, then cut it into ½-inch cubes. In a bowl, toss the squash with the olive oil and season with salt and pepper. Arrange the squash in one layer on a baking sheet and bake for 25 to 30 minutes, turning twice, until the cubes are golden brown around the edges and the flesh is fork-tender. Remove from the oven and let cool.

2 In a skillet, melt the butter over medium heat, watching carefully. As the foam subsides and the butter begins to brown, add the sage leaves and cook, stirring gently, until the sage is crisp and the butter is golden brown, 1 to 2 minutes. Remove from the heat.

☞ CONTINUED

3 In a large pot of salted boiling water, cook the pasta until al dente, 7 to 10 minutes. Drain.

4 In a large bowl, toss the pasta with the squash and the sage and browned butter. Season with salt and pepper. Scoop into warmed shallow bowls, sprinkle with the garlic chips, and serve immediately.

Serves 6 as a first course, or 4 as an entrée

GEMELLI WITH ARUGULA PESTO

rugula is the racy little sister of spinach: green and tender, with a sassy, peppery kick. We like to think of this concoction of pesto and pasta as comfort food with sass.

½ cup extra-virgin olive oil

1½ cups firmly packed baby arugula

3 cloves garlic, coarsely chopped

¼ cup (1 ounce) grated Parmesan cheese

¼ cup pine nuts

Salt and freshly ground black pepper

1 pound gemelli pasta

½ cup oven-roasted tomatoes *(page 158)*

1 teaspoon red pepper flakes

1 In a blender or food processor, combine the olive oil and arugula and process at medium speed for 1 to 2 minutes, until blended. Add the garlic and blend until nearly smooth. Add the Parmesan and the pine nuts, pulsing a few times so that the nuts remain coarsely ground. Season with salt and pepper.

2 In a large pot of salted boiling water, cook the pasta for 7 to 10 minutes, until al dente. Drain.

3 Pour the pesto over the pasta and toss to coat it completely. Stir in the tomatoes and red pepper flakes. Serve at once.

Serves 4

GNOCCHI WITH GORGONZOLA, ASPARAGUS & PINE NUTS

In ancient Egypt, garlic was highly regarded as a symbol of the cosmos because of its shape: a cohesive round made up of many smaller, individual parts. Egyptian historians note that the first strike among pyramid builders was due to a garlic shortage! Given the wide availability of garlic today, we don't have to worry about running out. To celebrate this abundance, we've paired potato dumplings, called gnocchi, with asparagus and creamy Gorgonzola to make a decadent dish.

2 pounds baking potatoes, scrubbed

1 large egg

1 teaspoon salt

½ teaspoon freshly ground black pepper

⅛ teaspoon ground nutmeg

2 cups all-purpose flour

½ cup pine nuts

GORGONZOLA–ASPARAGUS SAUCE

6 to 8 spears asparagus, trimmed

1 tablespoon plus ½ teaspoon olive oil

2 cloves garlic, coarsely chopped

¼ cup dry white wine

2 tablespoons heavy cream

2 ounces Gorgonzola cheese

Salt and freshly ground black pepper

☛ CONTINUED

1 Preheat the oven to 425°F. With a sharp fork, pierce the potatoes several times. Place on a baking sheet and bake until soft and tender, about 45 minutes. Remove from the oven and let cool to the touch. Cut the warm potatoes in half lengthwise and scoop the flesh into a bowl, discarding the skins. Press the potatoes through a potato ricer, then spread them on a baking sheet and let cool completely.

2 In a small bowl, beat the egg, salt, pepper, and nutmeg together. Put the potatoes in a bowl and add the egg mixture, stirring with a fork to blend. Put 1 cup of the flour into a sifter and sift over the top of the potato mixture, stirring gently to combine. Repeat with the second cup of flour. Do not overmix, or the dough will become sticky and difficult to handle.

3 Wash and dry your hands, dusting your palms lightly with flour. Divide the dough into 8 equal pieces. On a lightly floured work surface, roll each piece into a ½-inch-diameter rope with your hands. Cut the dough into little dumplings at 1-inch intervals. With the back of a fork, press lightly against the center of each dumpling to make gentle grooves.

4 Cook the gnocchi immediately or arrange them on a baking sheet so that they don't touch and place in the refrigerator. (If making the gnocchi more than a day in advance, freeze them on a baking sheet, then transfer to and store in a resealable plastic bag.) To cook the gnocchi, bring a large pot of water to a boil and add a generous amount of salt. Drop about half of the gnocchi into the pot two or three at a time, stirring once with a wooden spoon. Cook until they rise to the surface of the water, about 1 minute. Using a slotted spoon, transfer to a bowl.

5 Heat the ½ teaspoon olive oil in a small skillet over medium-low heat. Add the pine nuts and stir constantly until golden brown, about 5 to 7 minutes.

6 To make the sauce: In a saucepan of salted boiling water, blanch the asparagus for 3 minutes. Using tongs, remove the spears from the boiling water and plunge into cold water. Drain and cut into 2-inch lengths.

7 In a large, heavy skillet, heat the 1 tablespoon olive oil over medium-low heat. Add the garlic and sauté for 2 to 3 minutes, or until golden brown around the edges. Add the wine to the pan and stir as the alcohol evaporates. Decrease the heat to low, add the asparagus pieces, then gradually pour in the cream. Crumble the Gorgonzola into the pan and cook, stirring, until the cheese is melted. Season with salt and pepper.

8 Add the cooked gnocchi to the pan and gently toss to coat and heat through, about 2 minutes. Remove from the heat. Divide the gnocchi among warmed shallow bowls, sprinkle with the pine nuts, and serve immediately.

Serves 4

SPICY LAMB RAVIOLI IN FUMET

Noses around your house will perk up when you're cooking this dish, so expect to have lots of company in the kitchen while you're at it! This is a favorite at the Stinking Rose, and no wonder: tender lamb pasta squares float in a light, buttery broth that becomes fragrant with the reserved lamb juices as it reduces in volume. It's just plain stinkin' good.

2 tablespoons canola oil

1 pound ground lamb

2 tablespoons olive oil

1 yellow onion, finely chopped

4 cloves garlic, minced

2 tablespoons grated Parmesan cheese

½ cup ricotta cheese

2 slices day-old bread

Leaves from 1 sprig rosemary, minced

1 teaspoon curry powder

½ teaspoon cayenne pepper

1 teaspoon salt

½ teaspoon freshly ground black pepper

4 ounces white or cremini mushrooms, finely chopped

Pasta dough *(page 163)*, or 1 pound wonton wrappers

1 egg beaten

1½ teaspoons water

☞ CONTINUED

FUMET

2 cups chicken broth

½ cup canned crushed tomatoes

½ teaspoon red pepper flakes

Salt and freshly ground black pepper

½ cup unsalted butter

Grated Parmesan cheese, for garnish

Julienned fresh basil leaves, for garnish

1 In a sauté pan, heat the canola oil over medium heat. Add the lamb and sauté for 8 to 10 minutes, until browned, breaking up the meat with a wooden spoon to keep it separated and crumbly. Remove from the heat and drain, reserving the juices.

2 In a small skillet, heat the olive oil over medium-low heat. Add the onion and garlic and sauté for 5 to 7 minutes, until golden brown and soft. Remove from the heat and let cool. In a food processor, combine the onion mixture, Parmesan, ricotta, bread, rosemary, curry powder, cayenne, salt, and pepper. Blend on medium-high speed for 1 minute, or until crumbly, not smooth. Transfer to a bowl and add the lamb and mushrooms. Stir to combine evenly.

3 If using the pasta dough, divide it into 4 equal pieces. Using a pasta machine, roll in progressively thinner increments up to and including the thinnest setting. Lay the sheets out on a floured board and cut into 3-inch-wide strips with a rolling ravioli cutter or a sharp knife. On half of the strips, place 1 tablespoon of filling at 3-inch intervals down

the center. Beat the egg and water together. Brush around the filling with the egg mixture and cover with another strip of pasta. With your fingers, press gently around the filling mounds to remove any air, then seal the strips around the edges with the tines of a fork. Cut between the mounds to make individual ravioli. If using wonton wrappers, simply place 1 tablespoon of filling in the center of each wrapper and cover with another wrapper. Moisten the edges with a fingertip dipped in water and crimp the edges firmly with the tines of a fork to seal the filling inside.

4 Lay the ravioli on a floured baking sheet in a single layer and place in the freezer for at least 30 minutes to firm the dough.

5 To make the fumet: In a saucepan, combine the reserved lamb juices, broth, tomatoes, and pepper flakes. Season with salt and pepper and bring to a boil over high heat. Decrease the heat to medium and cook to reduce the broth by half, about 15 minutes. Add the butter and stir until it is completely melted.

6 Bring a large pot of water to a boil over high heat and salt generously. One by one, gently drop the ravioli into the water. Decrease the heat to medium and cook for 4 to 5 minutes, until the edges are tender and they float on the surface of the water. Gently drain and place into warmed soup bowls. Ladle the broth over the top and sprinkle with the Parmesan and basil. Serve at once.

Serves 4 to 6

VEGETABLE LASAGNA WITH POMODORO CREAM SAUCE

A legend from the Middle East says that when Satan left the Garden of Eden, onions sprang up from his left footprint, and garlic from his right. This lasagna is packed with lots of both, plus many other veggies, all held together with a tomato cream sauce that is simultaneously light and silky. You can thank the guy with the horns.

POMODORO CREAM SAUCE

I tablespoon olive oil

3 cloves garlic, minced

¼ cup diced yellow onion

2 tablespoons unsalted butter

I (14.5-ounce) can crushed tomatoes

I tablespoon minced fresh flat-leaf parsley

¾ cup water

2 tablespoons tomato paste

I teaspoon minced fresh thyme

Salt and freshly ground black pepper

½ cup heavy cream

I cup finely diced eggplant

I cup finely diced yellow bell pepper

 CONTINUED

1 cup finely diced yellow onion

½ teaspoon red pepper flakes

1 cup finely diced white mushrooms (about 6 ounces)

6 ounces shiitake mushrooms, stemmed and finely diced

1½ pounds pasta dough *(page 163)*, or 1 (16-ounce) package
   no-boil lasagna noodles

1 cup baby spinach leaves

1 pound mozzarella cheese, shredded

½ cup (2 ounces) grated Parmesan cheese

2 tablespoons chopped fresh basil

1 To make the sauce: Preheat the oven to 350°F. In a large, heavy skillet, heat the olive oil over medium-low heat and sauté the garlic and onion for 3 to 4 minutes, until golden brown. Stir in the butter until melted. Add the tomatoes, parsley, water, tomato paste, and thyme one at a time, stirring after each addition. Season with salt and pepper. Decrease the heat to low and simmer for 45 minutes to 1 hour, until thickened and flavorful. Remove from the heat and let cool for a few minutes, then add the cream, beating vigorously with a wire whisk to incorporate.

2 In a large bowl, combine the eggplant, bell pepper, onion, and mushrooms. Stir to blend.

3 If making your own pasta, divide the dough into 6 pieces and roll each piece through a pasta machine in progressively thinner sheets until you have used the thinnest setting. On a floured work surface, cut the pasta sheets into strips 3 inches wide and 9 inches long.

4 To assemble the lasagna: Spread ⅔ cup of the sauce over the bottom of a 9 by 13-inch baking dish. Cover the bottom of the dish with one layer of the pasta. Scatter one-third of the vegetable mixture over the pasta, then sprinkle with one-third of the spinach. Spoon ⅔ cup of the sauce over the spinach. Sprinkle with one-third of the mozzarella and 2 tablespoons of the Parmesan cheese. Repeat to make a total of three layers. On the last layer, top the cheese with a layer of pasta, then spread the remaining sauce over the top of the pasta.

5 Cover the dish with aluminum foil and bake for 1 hour. Remove the foil and sprinkle the remaining 2 tablespoons Parmesan over the top. Return to the oven uncovered and bake for 10 minutes, or until the cheese is golden brown and the lasagna is bubbly.

6 Remove from the oven and let cool for about 15 minutes. Cut into squares and sprinkle with the basil. Serve hot.

Serves 6 to 8

NORTH BEACH LASAGNA 👉

This is the type of rich, hearty lasagna that the original gangsters were likely to have dined on as they sat around a table in the back of a dim restaurant, smoking cigars and hatching shadowy plans. We could have called this the Al Capone Lasagna, but we decided to go with the name North Beach, just, ya know, to keep things copasetic.

I tablespoon olive oil

3 cloves garlic, minced

I large yellow onion, diced

I pound ground pork

I pound ground beef

Leaves from I sprig rosemary, minced

Leaves from 2 sprigs oregano, minced, or I teaspoon dried oregano, crumbled

I teaspoon aniseeeds

I (14.5-ounce) can crushed tomatoes

Salt and freshly ground black pepper

I½ pounds pasta dough (*page 163*), or I (16-ounce) package no-boil lasagna noodles

I pound mozzarella cheese, shredded

½ cup (2 ounces) grated Parmesan cheese

2 tablespoons chopped fresh basil

1 Preheat the oven to 350°F. In a large, heavy skillet, heat the olive oil over medium-low heat and sauté the garlic and onion for 3 to 4 minutes, until golden brown. Add the ground pork and ground beef and cook, breaking up the meat with a wooden spoon to distribute the heat evenly. Crumble the rosemary, oregano, and aniseeds into the meat and sauté for 15 to 20 minutes, until the meat is cooked through. Add the tomatoes and decrease the heat to low. Season with salt and pepper and simmer 10 to 15 minutes longer to meld the flavors.

2 If making your own pasta, divide the dough into 6 pieces and roll each piece through a pasta machine in progressively thinner sheets until you have used the thinnest setting. On a floured work surface, cut the pasta sheets into strips 3 inches wide and 9 inches long.

3 To assemble the lasagna, spread a scant amount of the meat sauce over the bottom of a 9 by 13-inch baking dish. Cover the bottom of the dish with a layer of pasta. Ladle one-third of the meat sauce over the pasta, then sprinkle with one-third of the mozzarella and 2 tablespoons of the Parmesan. Repeat to make a total of three layers. On the last layer, top the cheese with a layer of pasta, then spread the remaining sauce over the top of the pasta.

4 Cover the dish with aluminum foil and bake for 1 hour. Remove the foil and sprinkle the remaining 2 tablespoons Parmesan over the top. Return to the oven uncovered and bake for 10 minutes longer, or until the cheese is golden brown and the lasagna is bubbly.

5 Remove from the oven and let cool for about 15 minutes. Cut into squares and sprinkle with the basil. Serve hot.

Serves 6 to 8

WHOLE
DUNGENESS
GARLIC
ROASTED
IN OUR
SECRET SAUCE

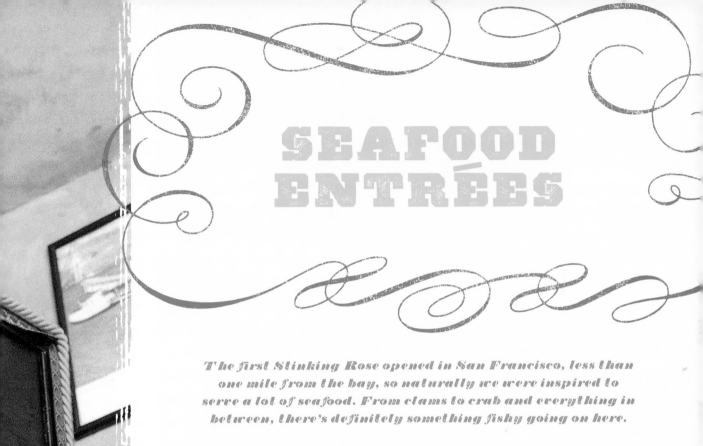

SEAFOOD ENTRÉES

The first Stinking Rose opened in San Francisco, less than one mile from the bay, so naturally we were inspired to serve a lot of seafood. From clams to crab and everything in between, there's definitely something fishy going on here.

~~~

GARLIC-ROASTED KILLER CRAB

Feeling crabby? We have just the cure. Garlic-Roasted Killer Crab is one of our signature dishes at the Stinking Rose. People come from all over the world to taste the finger-licking sauce that covers this delectable crustacean. We use only premium fresh Dungeness crabs; their sweet, tender meat is incomparable. October through May is the best time to find Dungeness crabs at your local fish market or grocer, but they can be found frozen during the off-season.

2 live or cooked Dungeness crabs (2-plus pounds each)

½ cup dry white wine

2 tablespoons olive oil

I shallot, minced

Leaves from I sprig thyme, minced

Leaves from I sprig rosemary, minced

2 tablespoons pink peppercorns

2 tablespoons canola oil

I tablespoon plus ½ teaspoon garlic salt

8 to 10 cloves roasted garlic (*page 155*), mashed

Minced fresh flat-leaf parsley, for garnish

1 If using live crabs, bring a large pot of water to a boil over high heat. Plunge the crabs into the boiling water and cook for about 10 minutes, or until they turn bright red. Remove the crabs from the pot and immerse in ice water for 3 to 4 minutes. Remove from the water.

☛ CONTINUED

2 To clean cooked crabs: Pull off the top shell of each crab; rinse the shells and reserve them. Turn the crabs over and pull off the triangular piece of shell and the spines beneath it; discard. Turn the crabs over again; pull off and discard the white gills on either side of the body. Remove and discard the white, crooked intestine in the center. Remove and discard the eyes and mouth parts. Remove and reserve the white and yellow crab "butter" in the body cavity and rinse the body cavity. Place the crabs shell side down in a baking dish. In a blender, process the crab "butter" with ¼ cup of the wine until smooth and creamy.

3 Preheat the oven to 325°F. In a heavy saucepan, heat the olive oil over medium heat. Add the shallot, thyme, rosemary, and peppercorns and sauté for about 5 minutes, or until the shallot is translucent. Stir in the remaining ¼ cup wine, then the canola oil, the 1 tablespoon garlic salt, and the crab "butter" mixture. Decrease the heat to low and simmer, stirring occasionally, for 10 minutes, or until the mixture is creamy and thick. Remove from the heat and skim any clumps from the top. Let cool for 3 to 4 minutes, then pass through a fine-meshed sieve and return to the saucepan. Add the mashed garlic cloves, stir well, then beat with a wire whisk until thick and creamy.

4 Ladle all but ¼ cup of the sauce over the crabs and roast for 15 to 20 minutes, until the crabmeat looks slightly dry and crisp on the top. Remove from the oven and arrange the crabs on a serving platter.

5 Drizzle 2 tablespoons of the remaining sauce over the exposed crab meat. Sprinkle with the ½ teaspoon garlic salt, then place the top shells back on the crab bodies. Brush the shells with a few drops of olive oil for a beautiful shine. Sprinkle the parsley over the whole platter and serve immediately, with the reserved sauce for dipping.

Serves 2 to 4

NOTE

Depending on where you buy your crabs, they could be live or cooked, so we've provided instructions for preparing them both ways. Read the recipe through once or twice before you begin; though it's not complicated, there are several steps and mini procedures along the way, so you'll want to have your wits about you. The final result is well worth it!

At the Stinking Rose, we tie bibs on people so they can recklessly crack and slurp without the worry of staining their clothes, and then we bring out hot, moistened hand towels at the end for easy cleanup. You might consider doing the same at home.

GARLIC-STEAMED MANILA CLAMS ☞

A big heap of steamed clams is the perfect way to end a day spent wandering the San Francisco streets in the cool, foggy air, so it isn't surprising that these are a favorite at the Stinking Rose. Luckily, the ingredients won't set you back too many clams, so you can whip up a batch yourself and remember the afternoon you drove down the crookedest street in the world or took the boat out to Alcatraz. Sop up the fragrant, garlicky broth with hunks of hot, crusty bread.

1 tablespoon olive oil

5 cloves garlic, coarsely chopped

2 shallots, minced

1 cup dry white wine

½ cup bottled clam juice

3 tablespoons unsalted butter

2 tablespoons minced fresh thyme

Freshly ground black pepper

2 pounds Manila or littleneck clams, scrubbed

2 tablespoons minced fresh flat-leaf parsley

1 In a deep, heavy saucepan, heat the olive oil over medium-low heat. Add the garlic and shallots and sauté for 3 to 4 minutes, until the shallots are translucent and the garlic is golden brown around the edges. Add the wine, clam juice, butter, and thyme and season with pepper. Increase the heat to high and bring the liquid to a boil; immediately add the clams and cover with a lid. Steam for 3 to 5 minutes, until the clam shells have

opened completely. Remove from the heat and discard any clams that have not opened.

2 To serve, divide the clams among warmed shallow bowls, ladle the broth over the top, then sprinkle with the parsley.

Serves 4

LEMON-BAKED SALMON WITH GARLIC-CAPER BUTTER

ncient legends say that if garlic appears in your dreams, it means that money is about to come your way. We think that you might be able to induce garlic float through your head while you sleep by dining on it beforehand. With that in mind, consider making this moist, flaky salmon fillet for dinner. It's topped with buttery sauce spiked with garlic and capers—just the thing to send you off to dreamland!!

GARLIC-CAPER BUTTER

¾ cup unsalted butter, at room temperature

2 tablespoons freshly squeezed lemon juice

1 tablespoon dry white wine

4 cloves garlic, minced

2 tablespoons capers

1 tablespoon minced fresh flat-leaf parsley

Salt and freshly ground black pepper

½ cup water

4 to 6 salmon fillets (6 to 8 ounces each)

1 lemon, rinsed and cut crosswise into thin wheels

1 tablespoon minced fresh flat-leaf parsley, for garnish

 CONTINUED

1 To make the caper butter: Preheat the oven to 325°F. In a blender or food processor, combine the butter, lemon juice, wine, and garlic. Pulse on low speed until smooth. Or, combine the ingredients in a bowl and whisk vigorously until smooth. Fold in the capers and half of the parsley. Season with salt and pepper.

2 Pour the water into a baking dish and place the salmon fillets in the dish, leaving 1 to 2 inches between them. Drizzle 1 tablespoon caper butter over each fillet and top with a wheel of lemon.

3 Bake for 15 minutes, or until the fillets are a dull pink on the outside and still rosy in the center. Remove from the oven and discard the lemon wheels.

4 Place on a serving platter, sprinkle with the remaining parsley, and garnish with the leftover lemon slices. Serve immediately, with the remaining caper butter on the side.

Serves 4 to 6

LOUISIANA SHRIMP IN A GARLIC-TOMATO BROTH

Isn't the term jumbo shrimp *something of a oxymoron? We're still scratching our heads at the term, but that doesn't stop us from liking the way they taste! At the Stinking Rose, we fly in freshwater shrimp from Louisiana for this dish, but that might be a bit tricky for those of you at home, so we recommend that you simply buy whatever fresh shrimp are available at your local market. We serve this in a heavy cast-iron pot for sharing at the table, but you can also divide it among individual bowls for serving.*

3 tablespoons olive oil

1 yellow onion, finely chopped

6 cloves garlic, minced

2 leaves fresh sage

1 (14.5-ounce) can chopped tomatoes with juice

1 teaspoon grated fresh ginger

1 cup bottled clam juice

1 teaspoon garlic salt

1 teaspoon red pepper flakes

1 tablespoon minced fresh flat-leaf parsley

Freshly ground black pepper

1 fennel bulb, trimmed, cored, and finely chopped

5 tablespoons unsalted butter

2 pounds jumbo shrimp (11 to 15 per pound) in the shell

 CONTINUED

1 In a heavy saucepan, heat the olive oil over medium-low heat. Add the onion and sauté, stirring occasionally, for about 10 minutes, or until the onion is translucent. Add the garlic and sauté for 3 to 4 minutes more, until the garlic turns a light golden color. Add the sage and sauté for 4 to 5 minutes, until the sage is crisp. Using the edge of a wooden spoon, break the sage into pieces in the pan.

2 Stir in the tomatoes and ginger, increase the heat to medium-high, and bring to a boil. Add the clam juice, garlic salt, pepper flakes, and parsley and season with pepper. Decrease the heat and simmer, uncovered, until the liquid is reduced by about one-fourth. Add the fennel and 4 tablespoons of the butter, stirring to melt the butter.

3 In a heavy skillet, melt the remaining 1 tablespoon butter over medium heat and add the shrimp, stirring them until they turn pink, about 3 minutes. Remove from the heat and immediately add the shrimp to the tomato broth. Ladle into a large bowl or individual bowls and serve at once.

Serves 4 to 6

BABY CLAMS & SHRIMP IN A COCONUT-CURRY BRODETTO

H ere, we took ideas from both Asian and Italian traditions and smacked them together, with scrumptious results. The word brodetto means a light broth, and this recipe combines tender shellfish in a creamy, Thai-inspired coconut curry broth that is at once delicate and flavorful. Be sure to have plenty of good, chewy bread to serve alongside; the sauce begs to be sopped up and savored to the very last drop.

1 tablespoon olive oil

1 small shallot, minced

2 cloves garlic, minced

1 (15-ounce) can coconut milk

2 cups bottled clam juice

Juice of 1 lime

1 tablespoon Madras curry powder

Salt and freshly ground black pepper

2 pounds baby clams in the shell

1 pound large shrimp (21 to 30 per pound), peeled and deveined, tails on

1 pint cherry tomatoes, halved

1 small bunch cilantro, stemmed and coarsely chopped

☞ CONTINUED

1 In a large cast-iron skillet, heat the olive oil over medium-low heat. Add the shallot and garlic and sauté for about 5 minutes, or until golden brown. Add the coconut milk, clam juice, and lime juice, stirring to combine thoroughly. Heat until bubbly and thick, about 10 minutes, then add the curry powder and season with salt and pepper.

2 Add the clams. When they begin to open, about 2 to 3 minutes, add the shrimp. Cook for 2 to 3 minutes more, until the shrimp have turned pink. Remove from the heat immediately and discard any clams that don't open.

3 Spoon the shellfish into warmed shallow bowls and ladle the curry broth over the top. Sprinkle with the cherry tomatoes and cilantro and serve at once.

Serves **4** to **6**

MUSSELS & LINGUIÇA IN A SAVORY BROTH

here are over three hundred varieties of garlic in existence! The "stinking rose" is grown on every continent and used by virtually every culture, but botanists agree that it was first found in Asia. This recipe was inspired by the tantalizing aroma of Asian noodle soup that wafts from Chinatown to North Beach. Linguiça sausage and mussels are simmered in a light broth with ginger, cilantro, and lime for an unexpected blend of flavors that bursts on the tongue. Serve with crostini or chewy bread to sop up the sauce.

1 tablespoon olive oil

1 pound linguiça sausages or hot Italian sausages, cut into
¼-inch-thick rounds

2 teaspoons minced fresh ginger

2 teaspoons minced garlic

1½ cups bottled clam juice

1 cup chicken broth

Juice of ½ lime

2 tablespoons tomato paste

2 pounds Prince Edward Island mussels, or other small to
medium mussels

1 small bunch cilantro, stemmed and coarsely chopped
(reserve 4 sprigs for garnish)

1 teaspoon red pepper flakes (optional)

 CONTINUED

1 In a sauté pan, heat the olive oil over medium heat. Add the sausage slices and cook for 5 to 7 minutes, tossing occasionally, until the sausage is cooked through and the edges are crisp. Decrease the heat to medium-low and stir in the ginger and garlic. Sauté for 1 minute, then stir in the clam juice, chicken broth, lime juice, and tomato paste. Cook until the clam juice begins to bubble, about 3 to 4 minutes. Add the mussels, cover, and cook for 2 to 3 minutes, until the mussel shells begin to open. Stir in the chopped cilantro and the pepper flakes and remove from the heat. Discard any mussels that don't open.

2 Divide the mussels among warmed shallow bowls and ladle the sausage and broth over them. Garnish each bowl with a sprig of cilantro and serve at once.

Serves 4

CIOPPINO

ioppino is an updated version of a classic Italian fish stew, chock-full of assorted fish and fragrant with fennel, garlic, and wine. Many years ago, when San Francisco fishermen added Dungeness crab, they called it cioppino, and the name stuck. Whatever you call it, it's absolutely wonderful. Consider the fish listed below as a recommendation; use whatever is local and in season. You can serve the stew a couple of different ways: alone; ladled over rice, pasta, or polenta; or alongside thickly sliced, toasted bread or taralli, the crunchy, ring-shaped Italian biscuits.

4 tablespoons olive oil

¼ cup chopped fennel

3 tablespoons chopped yellow onion

3 tablespoons minced shallots

3 cloves garlic, minced

¼ cup dry white wine

1 (28-ounce) can crushed tomatoes

2 tablespoons minced fresh flat-leaf parsley

1 teaspoon red pepper flakes

1 cup bottled clam juice

1 cup water

Salt and freshly ground black pepper

½ cup unsalted butter

8 ounces Prince Edward Island mussels

8 ounces Manila or littleneck clams

CONTINUED

1 (8-ounce) white fish fillet (such as halibut, cod, or tilapia), cut into chunks

4 ounces cleaned calamari (*see page 19*), cut into 1-inch-wide rings

4 ounces large shrimp (21 to 30 per pound), peeled and deveined, tails on

2 tablespoons minced fresh basil

Fennel fronds, for garnish

1 In a large, heavy saucepan, heat 2 tablespoons of the olive oil over medium-low heat. Add the chopped fennel, onion, shallots, and garlic and sauté for 4 to 5 minutes, until golden brown. Stir in the wine, then the tomatoes, parsley, pepper flakes, clam juice, and water. Season with salt and pepper. Bring to a boil over high heat, then decrease the heat to low and simmer for 30 minutes. Add the butter and stir to melt, then remove from the heat.

2 In a large cast-iron skillet, heat the remaining 2 tablespoons olive oil over medium heat and toss in the mussels and clams. Cook for 4 minutes. As the mussels and clams begin to open, add the fillet, calamari, and shrimp and sprinkle with salt and pepper. Sauté for 2 to 3 minutes, until the shrimp turn pink. Discard any mussels or clams that don't open. Add 1 cup of the tomato mixture and simmer for 5 minutes. Transfer the contents of the skillet to the saucepan with the remaining tomato mixture and simmer for 2 to 3 minutes.

3 Ladle into soup bowls. Sprinkle with the basil, garnish with the fennel fronds, and serve immediately.

Serves 4 to 6

HAWAIIAN SUNFISH WITH CHERRY TOMATOES, ROASTED GARLIC & OLIVES 👉

Hawaiian sunfish is the common restaurant name for tilapia (pronounced teh-LAH-pee-uh), a white fish with a tender, flaky texture and delicate flavor. It has been suggested that perhaps this "perch of the Nile" was the fish that Jesus multiplied when he fed the crowds in the famous story of the loaves and fishes, but we can't guarantee it. Tilapia has become widely available in the past couple of years, so you should have no problem locating it at the fish counter of your local market.

2 tablespoons olive oil

4 tilapia fillets (5 to 7 ounces each)

Salt and freshly ground black pepper

1 pint cherry tomatoes in various colors, halved

½ cup kalamata olives, pitted and halved

¼ cup roasted garlic cloves (*page 155*)

2 tablespoons chopped fresh basil

1 In a cast-iron skillet, heat 1 tablespoon of the olive oil over very high heat until the surface shimmers. Season the fillets with salt and pepper on both sides and sear for 2 minutes on each side, or until nicely browned on the outside and opaque throughout. Transfer to a warmed platter.

2 In another skillet, heat the remaining 1 tablespoon olive oil over medium heat and sauté the cherry tomatoes, olives, and roasted garlic for 1 minute to heat them through.

3 Spoon the tomato mixture over the fish and sprinkle with the basil. Serve immediately.

Serves 4

Chicago Daily Tribune

DEWEY DEFEATS TRUMAN

G.O.P. Sweep Indicated in State; Boyle Leads in City

HEARTY ENTRÉES

When you're in the mood to chow down, look no further. Even the most ravenous appetite will be sated with our juicy prime rib or porterhouse pork chop. So go ahead: dig in.

FORTY-CLOVE GARLIC CHICKEN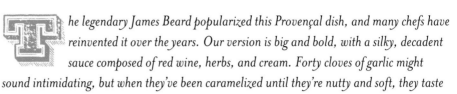

The legendary James Beard popularized this Provençal dish, and many chefs have reinvented it over the years. Our version is big and bold, with a silky, decadent sauce composed of red wine, herbs, and cream. Forty cloves of garlic might sound intimidating, but when they've been caramelized until they're nutty and soft, they taste divine! Serve with Pesto Mashed Potatoes (page 134).

1 large (2½- to 3-pound) broiler-fryer chicken

MARINADE

2 tablespoons olive oil
2 tablespoons minced garlic
Leaves from 1 sprig rosemary, minced
Salt and freshly ground black pepper

SAUCE

1 cup dry red wine
1 shallot, quartered
4 cloves garlic, chopped
Leaves from 1 sprig rosemary, minced
Leaves from 2 sprigs thyme, minced
1¼ cups heavy cream
½ cup unsalted butter, cut into chunks
Salt and freshly ground black pepper

1½ cups roasted garlic cloves (page 155)

CONTINUED

1 Remove the giblets from the chicken and reserve for another use. With a large, sharp knife, cut the chicken in half lengthwise, then cut in half crosswise to separate the breast from the thighs.

2 To make the marinade: Combine all the ingredients in a small bowl. Put the chicken parts in a heavy resealable plastic bag, pour the marinade over the chicken, and seal the bag. Work your hands over the bag until the liquid covers all the chicken parts. Place the bag in the refrigerator for 1 to 3 hours.

3 To make the sauce: In a heavy saucepan, combine the wine, shallot, garlic, rosemary, and thyme. Bring to a boil over high heat, then decrease the heat to medium-low and cook, stirring occasionally, for 2 to 3 minutes. Gradually stir in the cream and cook to reduce the liquid by one-third, about 10 minutes. Add the butter in batches, stirring to melt. Season with salt and pepper. Pass the sauce through a fine-meshed sieve, cover, and set aside.

4 Preheat the oven to 350°F. Put the chicken in a heavy baking dish and bake for 20 minutes. Remove from the oven, turn the chicken pieces over, and baste with the pan juices. Return to the oven and bake for another 20 minutes, or until the skin is crackly and golden brown and the meat is opaque throughout.

5 Arrange the chicken on a serving platter. Pour the warm sauce over the chicken and sprinkle with the roasted garlic cloves. Serve immediately.

Serves 4

CHICKEN CACCIATORE IN BLACK OLIVE & TOMATO SAUCE 👉

arlic has long been lauded for its aphrodisiac qualities, an attribute that we think everyone should know about! The next time you want to prepare a romantic meal, consider this classic cacciatore with hot garlicky pasta. Pair with a nice red wine and—voila!—dinner is served. What happens afterward is up to you.

1 (3-pound) chicken, cut into pieces

Salt and freshly ground black pepper

5 tablespoons olive oil

1 white onion, finely chopped

2 cloves garlic, minced

½ cup dry red wine

1½ pounds Roma tomatoes, coarsely chopped, or
   2 (14.5-ounce) cans crushed tomatoes

½ cup kalamata olives, pitted

¾ cup chicken broth

1 tablespoon minced fresh rosemary

Garlic Noodles (*page 130*), for serving

2 tablespoons chopped fresh basil

👉 **CONTINUED**

1 Preheat the oven to 375°F. Sprinkle the chicken with salt and pepper. In a heavy, ovenproof skillet, heat 2 tablespoons of the olive oil over high heat. Add the chicken and sauté for 5 minutes on each side, or until golden brown. Transfer the chicken to a bowl.

2 Decrease the heat to medium-low. Add the onion and garlic to the skillet and sauté for about 5 minutes, or until golden brown. Add the wine and stir to scrape up the browned bits from the bottom of the pan. Decrease the heat to medium and add the tomatoes, olives, and broth. Simmer for 4 to 5 minutes to blend the flavors.

3 Return the chicken to the skillet. Sprinkle with the rosemary and drizzle with the remaining 3 tablespoons olive oil. Place the skillet in the oven and roast the chicken, uncovered, for 25 to 35 minutes, until the juices run clear when the flesh is pierced with a knife.

4 Remove the skillet from the oven. Place the pasta in a shallow serving bowl and arrange the chicken on top. Ladle the sauce over the chicken and noodles and sprinkle with the basil. Serve immediately.

Serves 4 to 6

GRILLED PORTOBELLO MUSHROOMS WITH SAUTÉED VEGETABLES

hough garlic has been a dietary staple around the world for centuries, America was slow to catch on. In the 1920s, before "gourmet" cooking appeared in America, garlic was thought to be the food of immigrants. Some of the names given to the bulb were Italian perfume, Bronx vanilla, and halitosis. Sounds appetizing, doesn't it? Good thing we can now enjoy garlic without shame. In this recipe, we grill whole portobello mushrooms and use them like boats to harbor a medley of delicious vegetables.

8 large (4- to 5-inch-diameter) portobello mushrooms,
   gills and stems removed

2 tablespoons olive oil

5 teaspoons coarsely chopped garlic

½ cup finely chopped red onion

I cup sliced baby zucchini

I cup finely chopped red bell pepper

I small eggplant, peeled and cut into ½-inch cubes

¼ cup plus I tablespoon balsamic vinegar

I tablespoon chopped fresh basil

I tablespoon minced fresh rosemary

Salt and freshly ground black pepper

2 tablespoons unsalted butter

1 Preheat the oven to 300°F. Line a baking sheet with aluminim foil.
Heat a grill pan or large, heavy skillet over high heat for about 3 minutes,

CONTINUED

until a drop of olive oil slides smoothly over the surface. Brush the tops of the mushrooms with 1 tablespoon of the olive oil, then place them, top side down, in the pan and sear for 1½ minutes. Turn and repeat on the other side, then remove from the pan. Overcooking on this step will result in soggy mushrooms, so watch the time carefully! Place 4 of the mushrooms on the prepared baking sheet, top side down. Place the other 4 on a plate.

2 Return the skillet to the stove top and heat the remaining 1 tablespoon olive oil over medium-low heat. Add the garlic and onion and sauté for 3 to 4 minutes, until translucent. Increase the heat to medium and add the zucchini, bell pepper, and eggplant and sauté for 7 to 9 minutes, until the vegetables begin to soften and wilt. Add the 1 tablespoon balsamic vinegar and toss the vegetables in the pan until they are coated with the vinegar and it begins to caramelize around the edges. Remove from the heat. Add the basil and rosemary and season with salt and pepper.

3 Divide the vegetable mixture among the mushrooms on the baking sheet, filling each mushroom. Set another mushroom on top of each one, top side up, as if you were placing the top bun on a hamburger.

4 Roast for 7 to 9 minutes, until heated through. Meanwhile, melt the butter in a heavy skillet over medium heat. Add the ¼ cup balsamic vinegar and cook to reduce by two-thirds.

5 Remove the mushrooms from the oven and carefully place each mushroom stack on a serving plate. Drizzle with the vinegar mixture and serve immediately.

Serves 4

ROASTED RABBIT WITH GARLIC & OLIVES 👉

hough some people report that rabbit tastes *"just like chicken,"* we think that it tastes exactly like rabbit. In this recipe, rabbit pieces are dredged in flour and browned, then baked until the meat is soft and succulent. Garlic cloves are roasted along with the rabbit until they are soft and sweet.

½ cup all-purpose flour

1 teaspoon salt

1 teaspoon freshly ground black pepper

2 rabbits, cleaned and cut into pieces

5 tablespoons extra-virgin olive oil

½ cup garlic cloves

½ cup pitted green olives (such as picholine or Spanish green olives)

Leaves from 3 sprigs thyme, chopped

1 Preheat the oven to 350°F. In a shallow bowl, stir the flour, salt, and pepper together. Dredge the rabbit pieces in the flour mixture, completely coating the meat on all sides.

2 In a large cast-iron skillet, heat 3 tablespoons of the olive oil over medium heat. Put the rabbit in the skillet and cook for 4 to 5 minutes on each side, until nicely browned.

3 In a small bowl, toss the garlic with 1 tablespoon of the olive oil to coat completely.

4 Transfer the rabbit to a baking dish and sprinkle with the garlic, olives, and thyme. Bake, uncovered, for about 1 hour, or until the garlic cloves are golden brown and the rabbit is browned on the outside and opaque throughout.

5 Drizzle the remaining 1 tablespoon olive oil in an abstract pattern on a serving platter and arrange the rabbit on top. Scoop the garlic cloves and olives from the baking dish and sprinkle over the rabbit. Serve immediately.

Serves 4

SILENCE OF THE LAMB SHANKS WITH CHIANTI GLAZE & FAVA BEANS 👉

We created this recipe in honor of Hannibal Lector, that deliciously nasty screen villain who dined on his victims with great relish. We don't want to have what he's having, but we hope you will enjoy this lamb shank that is falling-off-the-bone tender, with a flavorful reduction of red wine and butter and the bright, springy crunch of fava beans. To your health!

2 tablespoons olive oil

2 tablespoons minced garlic

1 tablespoon minced fresh rosemary

1 teaspoon salt

1 teaspoon freshly ground black pepper

4 lamb shanks (12 to 16 ounces each)

3 cups beef broth, plus more as needed

1 pound fava beans, shelled

¾ cup Chianti or other dry red wine

2 tablespoons unsalted butter

1 In a small bowl, combine the olive oil, garlic, rosemary, salt, and pepper. Put the lamb shanks into in a large resealable plastic bag and add the marinade. Seal the bag and work your hands over the shank pieces until the liquid covers all of the meat. Marinate in the refrigerator for at least 2 hours.

2 Preheat the oven to 300°F. Put the lamb shanks in a heavy roasting pan, pour the marinade over, and add beef broth to cover. Bake, uncovered, for 2½ to 3 hours, until the meat is tender.

3 Shortly before removing the lamb from the oven, prepare the fava beans. In a large pot of salted boiling water, blanch the beans for 2 to 3 minutes. Drain the beans and plunge them into ice water. Peel the beans by pinching the skin at one end of each bean and removing it.

4 Transfer the lamb to a serving platter and cover loosely with an aluminim foil tent. Let the pan juices cool for a few moments, then strain through a fine-mesh sieve. Pour into a skillet and cook over medium heat to reduce by half, about 7 to 10 minutes. Add the Chianti, then stir in the butter and cook until velvety and thick, about 3 minutes.

5 Pour the Chianti glaze over the lamb shanks and sprinkle the fava beans over the top. Serve hot.

Serves 4

SLOW-ROASTED PRIME RIB ENCRUSTED WITH SEA SALT, GARLIC & HERBS

his is a recipe for all you carnivores out there. You'll begin with a big hunk of prime rib roast, slather it with garlic and herbs, and roast it ever so slowly until the meat is juicy and medium-rare. We recommend that you whip up a batch of Creamy Garlic-Spinach Cheese Fondue (page 20) to sate your hunger pangs while this is in the oven. Horseradish fans should try a dollop of two parts prepared horseradish to one part sour cream atop each slice of roast.

½ cup olive oil

8 cloves garlic, minced

2 tablespoons minced fresh rosemary

1 tablespoon minced fresh thyme

½ cup coarse sea salt

2 teaspoons freshly ground black pepper

1 (6-pound) boneless prime rib beef roast

⅓ cup dry white wine

1 cup beef broth

1 Preheat the oven to 300°F. In a small bowl, combine the olive oil, garlic, rosemary, thyme, salt, and pepper and stir to form a thick, chunky mixture. Put the rib roast in a roasting pan and pour the herb mixture over the top, rubbing it into the meat with your hands until the entire roast is covered with bits of garlic and herbs. Be sure that the sea salt is scattered all over the surface of the roast.

☛ CONTINUED

2 Roast for 3½ to 4 hours, until an instant-read thermometer inserted in the center of the roast registers 135°F for medium-rare. If the crust browns too quickly, tent the roast loosely with aluminum foil. Remove from the oven. Transfer the roast to a platter and cover it loosely with aluminum foil.

3 Pour the pan juices into a glass measuring cup and place in the freezer for 10 minutes. Scrape the congealed fat off of the top, returning the juices plus 1 tablespoon of the fat to the pan. (Or, use a fat separator.) Place the roasting pan over medium heat, stirring to scrape up the browned bits from the bottom of the pan. Add the wine and broth and simmer to reduce the liquid by half. Season with pepper.

4 Carve the roast and serve with the pan sauce.

Serves 8

GARLIC-BRAISED BONELESS BEEF SHORT RIBS

L egend has it that the Romans used to gnaw on raw garlic before battle to give them the edge over their enemies. We wonder whether it was effective because of its innate powers or because their breath knocked over the soldiers on the opposing side! In honor of those valiant warriors, we've created a dish that is sure to put hair on your chest. Big hunks of meat! Lots of garlic! Grrr. Beef short ribs are easy to find at your local meat counter; look for an even, bright color and moist rib bones. The secret to achieving a rich, intense flavor in this dish is the braising step, so be sure not to skip it!

3 to 4 pounds boneless beef short ribs

Garlic salt and freshly ground black pepper

3 tablespoons olive oil

4 cups beef broth

Leaves from 3 sprigs thyme, coarsely chopped

6 cloves garlic

4 sprigs rosemary

½ cup dry white wine

2 tablespoons unsalted butter

1 Preheat the oven to 350°F. Season the short ribs with the garlic salt and black pepper. In a large cast-iron skillet or Dutch oven, heat the olive oil over high heat until it begins to smoke then sear the ribs for 3 to 4 minutes on each side, until browned on the edges. Remove from the heat.

 CONTINUED

Add the broth, thyme, and garlic. Insert the rosemary sprigs between the short ribs and cover the pan with aluminum foil. Place in the oven and bake for 1 hour and 45 minutes, until the meat is very tender and nearly falls apart when prodded lightly with a fork. Turn off the heat and let the meat rest in the oven for about 30 minutes.

2 Remove the pan from the oven. Using a slotted spoon, transfer the ribs to a deep platter. Remove the garlic cloves and reserve for another use (such as Garlic Mashed Potatoes, page 131).

3 Place the skillet over medium heat; add the wine and stir to scrape up the browned bits from the bottom of the pan. Stir in the butter and cook, stirring frequently, for 5 to 7 minutes, until the sauce is velvety and thick. Remove from the heat and pour the sauce over the short ribs. Serve immediately.

Serves 4 to 6

PORK CHOPS WITH GARLIC RELISH & CARAMELIZED APPLES ☛

*T*here are hundreds of guesses as to when garlic first made its appearance in the world. It has been suggested that the apple that tempted Eve in the Garden of Eden was, in fact, a bulb of garlic, but we haven't been able to verify that yet. What we have done is to combine the flavors of garlic and apples for a result that is sinfully delicious. Serve with Garlic Mashed Potatoes (page 131).

GARLIC RELISH

1 cup champagne vinegar

16 to 20 cloves garlic

½ cup sugar

1 tablespoon red pepper flakes

2 tablespoons finely chopped red bell pepper

CARAMELIZED APPLES

3 tablespoons unsalted butter

2 Fuji apples, peeled, cored, and cut into ¼-inch wedges

¼ cup sugar

1 tablespoon brandy

4 to 6 double-cut pork chops

Salt and freshly ground black pepper

1 tablespoon olive oil

☛ CONTINUED

1 Preheat the oven to 350°F. To make the relish: In a heavy saucepan, combine the vinegar, garlic, sugar, and pepper flakes. Bring to a simmer over low heat and cook for 8 to 10 minutes, until the garlic cloves are soft. Stir in the bell pepper and simmer for 3 to 4 minutes. Remove from the heat and let cool.

2 To make the caramelized apples: In a heavy saucepan, melt the butter over medium heat, then stir in the apples. Sprinkle the sugar over the apples and stir again. Cook, stirring every minute or so, until the sugar caramelizes and the apples are coated with a light brown glaze. Stir in the brandy, then remove from the heat.

3 Season both sides of each pork chop with salt and pepper. In a large cast-iron skillet, heat the olive oil over high heat until the surface shimmers and sear the pork chops until lightly browned, about 2 minutes on each side. Transfer to a baking dish, placing the chops in one layer. Cover with aluminum foil and bake for 25 to 30 minutes, until the juices run clear when the chops are pierced with a knife. Turn the oven off and leave the baking dish in the oven 5 minutes longer.

4 Transfer the pork chops to a platter. Arrange the caramelized apples to one side and spoon the relish over the chops. Serve immediately.

Serves 4 to 6

RIB-EYE STEAKS WITH GARLIC & ROSEMARY ☞

Will Rogers once commented that at harvesttime, Gilroy, California (home of the Gilroy Garlic Festival), is "the only town in America where you can marinate a steak just by hanging it out on the clothesline." Since that probably won't work where you live, you might want to try marinating your steak the Stinking Rose way. You don't need fancy equipment to make a great steak at home, just a really good cut of meat. Select a thick, tender steak with a nice amount of marbling; don't worry, a lot of the fat will cook off, and what is left will keep the meat tender and delicious.

> 2 large cloves garlic, halved
> 4 (10-ounce) rib-eye steaks
> Salt and freshly ground black pepper
> 2 sprigs rosemary
> ¼ cup dry white wine
> 2 tablespoons butter

1 Rub the cut edge of 1 garlic half over the interior of a large cast-iron skillet.

2 Set the skillet over medium heat. Lightly sprinkle the steaks with salt and pepper on both sides and add the steaks to the skillet. Place all the garlic and a sprig of rosemary on one side of the skillet to add just a hint of flavor.

3 Cook the steaks on the first side for 3 to 4 minutes, then turn and cook another 6 or 7 minutes for medium-rare (for a 1½-inch-thick steak). Once the rosemary and garlic begin to brown, remove them from the pan.

4 Transfer the steaks to warmed plates. Add the wine and butter to the skillet, stirring to scrape up the browned bits from the bottom of the pan. When the mixture starts to bubble, remove from the heat and drizzle over the top of the steaks. Serve immediately.

Serves 4

GARLIC-ENCRUSTED BABY BACK RIBS

 hen customers walk through the door of the Stinking Rose singing "I want my baby-back, baby-back, baby-back . . . " we know just what to do! These tender, flavorful ribs are encrusted with fresh rosemary and loads of garlic (but of course!) and baked until the meat quite literally falls off the bone. We recommend serving these with a big green salad, and with a nice bottle of Chianti to wash it all down.

¼ cup olive oil

10 cloves garlic, minced

Leaves from 3 sprigs rosemary, coarsely chopped

2 teaspoons sugar

2 tablespoons white wine vinegar

1 teaspoon salt

1 teaspoon freshly ground black pepper

4 pounds baby back pork ribs (about 4 racks)

½ cup Barbecue Sauce (page 42)

1 In a bowl, stir the olive oil, garlic, rosemary, sugar, vinegar, salt, and pepper together.

2 Put the ribs in a shallow baking dish. With a fork or paring knife, pierce the meat all over to allow the marinade to penetrate. Pour the olive oil mixture over the ribs, rubbing it into the meat with your hands so

☞ CONTINUED

that the ribs are entirely coated with the garlic and herbs. Cover the dish and refrigerate for at least 3 hours or overnight.

3 Preheat the oven to 275°F. Transfer the ribs to a baking dish large enough to hold them all in one layer. Reserve the marinade. Brush both sides of the ribs with the barbecue sauce, then arrange them meat side up in the dish. Roast on the middle rack of the oven, basting with the marinade, for about 2½ hours, or until the meat is cooked through and very tender, easily separating from the bone when prodded with a fork.

4 Increase the oven temperature to 500°F. Cook for an additional 15 minutes to make the outer edges of the ribs crisp. Remove from the oven, cut the ribs into sections, and serve.

Serves 4

ITALIAN MEAT LOAF

his is most definitely not your mother's meat loaf! We have created a decidedly nontraditional sauce with the deep, smoky flavor of ancho chili powder and perfectly accented with bittersweet chocolate and a hint of cream.

1 tablespoon olive oil

½ cup finely diced carrots

½ cup finely diced celery

½ cup finely diced white or yellow onion

4 eggs

1 cup rolled oats

½ cup ketchup

2 tablespoons Worcestershire sauce

¼ cup roasted garlic cloves (*page 155*), gently mashed

2½ pounds ground chuck

1½ teaspoons salt

Freshly ground black pepper

SAUCE

1 cup tomato juice

¾ cup veal stock or beef broth

½ cup ketchup

1 tablespoon unsalted butter

2 tablespoons sugar

 CONTINUED

1 teaspoon ancho chili powder
1 tablespoon grated bittersweet chocolate
2 tablespoons heavy cream
Salt and freshly ground black pepper

1 Preheat the oven to 350°F. In a cast-iron skillet, heat the olive oil over medium heat. Add the carrots, celery, and onion and sauté for 5 minutes, or until the celery is translucent and the onion is golden brown. Remove from the heat.

2 In a large bowl, combine the sautéed vegetables, eggs, oats, ketchup, Worcestershire sauce, and roasted garlic. Stir to blend, then add the ground chuck and blend the mixture well with a large spoon or your hands. Season with the salt and pepper.

3 In an oiled large baking dish, form the mixture into a loaf, patting it into a shape that is roughly even on all sides. Place the pan on the middle rack of the oven and bake, uncovered, for 1 hour or until an instant-read thermometer inserted in the center of the loaf registers 160°F.

4 To make the sauce: In a small saucepan, combine the tomato juice, stock, and ketchup. Place over medium heat and simmer for 15 to 20 minutes, until thick and bubbly.

5 In a separate saucepan, melt the butter over low heat and add the sugar and ancho chili powder. Gradually add the chocolate, stirring until melted, then add the cream and stir until the mixture is fully blended. Remove from the heat.

6 Whisk the chocolate mixture into the tomato sauce until smooth. Season with salt and pepper.

7 Cut the meat loaf into slices and serve on warmed plates, with the sauce on the side.

Serves 6 to 8

ON THE SIDE

Would you like some garlic with your garlic? These dishes are chock-full of flavor and garlicky goodness. We like to serve our side dishes family style, which means that everyone can get a bite of this or a taste of that. Not that you have to share; we're just saying that you might want to.

CRUNCHY MARINATED CAULIFLOWER SALAD

n old Yiddish proverb says: "Three nickels will get you on the subway, but garlic will get you a seat." This recipe might encourage you to give it a try! We've taken that pale white vegetable and turned it into something that is worth fighting over the last piece. Or the last seat, depending on where you're at.

1 cauliflower, separated into smallish florets

2 tablespoons extra-virgin olive oil

1 clove garlic, shaved into paper-thin slivers

½ teaspoon dried oregano

1 teaspoon red pepper flakes

1 teaspoon coarse sea salt

1 lemon, halved

Freshly ground black pepper

1 Fill a bowl half full with ice cubes and add cold water to cover. In a saucepan of salted boiling water, cook the cauliflower for 5 to 7 minutes, until crisp-tender. Using a slotted spoon, transfer the cauliflower to the ice-water bath. Let stand until cool, about 3 to 4 minutes. Drain and pat dry.

2 In a bowl, combine the cauliflower, olive oil, garlic, oregano, pepper flakes, and salt and toss to coat. Squeeze the lemon juice over the salad and season with pepper. Let stand for 30 minutes at room temperature to blend the flavors before serving.

Serves 4 to 6

EGGPLANT & CARAMELIZED ONIONS WITH ROQUEFORT DRESSING ☞

*H*ere's a little experiment you might try at home to test the powers of garlic: rub the cut edge of a clove against your bare foot. In seconds, the taste of garlic will appear in your mouth! For a more satisfying investigation, try this recipe that combines the meatiness of eggplant with the caramely sweetness of onion and the pungent tang of Roquefort cheese. Serve it as a side dish, or use it to top a pizza or slide into a sandwich.

2 teaspoons white wine vinegar

1 unpeeled yellow onion

4 unpeeled cloves garlic

¼ cup plus 1 tablespoon extra-virgin olive oil

1 eggplant, cut lengthwise into ¼-inch-thick slices

3 tablespoons best-quality balsamic vinegar

¼ cup (1 ounce) crumbled Roquefort cheese

Juice of ½ lemon

Salt and freshly ground black pepper

1 Preheat the oven to 250°F. Pour ½ inch water into a small baking dish, add the white vinegar, and place the onion and garlic cloves in the center. Roast for 45 minutes to 1 hour, until the onion is very soft and the outer papery layers of both the onion and garlic are crisp and brown.

2 Meanwhile, in a grill pan or heavy skillet, heat 1 tablespoon of the olive oil over medium-high heat and sear the eggplant slices for 3 to 4 minutes on each side, until golden brown and soft. Using a metal spatula, transfer to paper towels to drain.

3 Remove the onion and garlic from the oven and let cool for about 5 minutes. Hold the onion over a bowl and squeeze gently, pushing out the soft, caramelized insides. Discard the husk and cut the insides into bite-sized pieces. Squeeze the garlic into the onion mixture, discarding the peels, and mash gently with the back of a spoon, stirring to combine the onion and garlic.

4 In a skillet, heat the balsamic vinegar over low heat and add the egg-plant and the onion mixture. Cook, stirring occasionally, for about 10 minutes, or until the cooking liquids have caramelized around the vegetables.

5 In a small bowl, stir the cheese, the ¼ cup olive oil, and the lemon juice together to make a thick, chunky dressing. Season with salt and pepper.

6 Arrange the eggplant slices and onion mixture on a plate and spoon the dressing over the top. Serve warm.

Serves 4

GARLIC NOODLES

Remember the scene in Lady and the Tramp *when the lovestruck pups are sucking on opposite ends of one piece of spaghetti in Tony's Diner? That's what this recipe reminds us of. Be sure to use imported Italian Parmesan cheese for optimal flavor. These noodles are a perfect accompaniment to Garlic-Roasted Killer Crab (page 74) or Forty-Clove Garlic Chicken (page 96).*

> 8 ounces dried thin ribbon pasta, such as spaghetti or tagliarini
> 2 tablespoons extra-virgin olive oil
> 3 cloves garlic, crushed
> I teaspoon red pepper flakes
> I teaspoon garlic salt
> I small bunch flat-leaf parsley, stemmed and minced
> 2 tablespoons grated Parmesan cheese

1 In a large pot of salted boiling water, cook the pasta for 8 to 10 minutes, until al dente. Drain and transfer to a bowl.

2 In a skillet over medium-low heat, heat the olive oil and garlic for I to 2 minutes, until fragrant, then add the pepper flakes and garlic salt. Pour over the pasta and toss to coat. Sprinkle with the parsley and cheese and toss again. Serve immediately.

Serves 2 to 4

GARLIC MASHED POTATOES ☞

These potatoes are something of a legend at the Stinking Rose. We use Yukon Gold potatoes for their creamy consistency and buttery golden color, and we add a couple of turnips for a hint of sweetness and depth. Serve these alongside any of the entrées in this book for a satisfying meal!

> 1 pound Yukon Gold potatoes, peeled and cubed
>
> 2 turnips, peeled and cubed
>
> ½ cup garlic cloves
>
> 3 tablespoons unsalted butter
>
> ½ cup heavy cream
>
> Salt
>
> 1 teaspoon freshly ground white pepper

1 In a heavy saucepan, combine the potatoes, turnips, and garlic. Add cold water to cover the vegetables. Bring to a boil over medium-high heat, then decrease the heat and simmer until the potatoes and turnips are soft, 15 to 20 minutes. Remove from the heat and drain.

2 Using a potato masher, mash the vegetables together in the pan until smooth. Or, use a potato ricer to purée them into a bowl. Immediately add the butter, stirring to melt, then gradually stir in the cream. For extra-fluffy potatoes, beat with a hand mixer for 2 to 3 minutes. Season with salt and the white pepper and serve immediately.

Serves 4

PESTO MASHED POTATOES

*W*here in the world can you find green mashed potatoes? At the Stinking Rose, of course! To create this colorful side dish, we first make pesto with garlic and loads of fresh basil and then mix it into buttery mashed potatoes for a delicious treat that looks great next to a platter of Forty-Clove Garlic Chicken (page 96) or Silence of the Lamb Shanks with Chianti Glaze and Fava Beans (page 106).

1½ pounds Yukon Gold potatoes, peeled and cubed

1 teaspoon salt

½ cup unsalted butter

PESTO

¼ cup extra-virgin olive oil

1 cup firmly packed basil leaves

3 cloves garlic, coarsely chopped

3 tablespoons pine nuts

¼ cup (1 ounce) grated Parmesan cheese

Salt and freshly ground black pepper

1 In a heavy saucepan, combine the potatoes, salt, and cold water to cover. Bring to a boil over medium-high heat, then decrease the heat to medium-low and simmer, uncovered, until the potatoes are soft, about 15 to 20 minutes.

2 Remove from the heat and drain. Add the butter and mash together with a potato masher until the butter is melted and incorporated into the potatoes. Cover and set aside.

3 To make the pesto: In a blender or food processor, combine the olive oil, basil, and garlic. Process on medium speed for 1 to 2 minutes, until smooth. Add the pine nuts and Parmesan cheese and pulse to blend. Season with salt and pepper.

4 Using a large rubber spatula, mix the pesto into the mashed potatoes until blended. Serve immediately.

Serves 4

ACINI DI PEPE WITH SUGAR SNAP PEAS

*A*cini di pepe is a tiny round Italian pasta whose name means "peppercorns." We love them at the Stinking Rose—they're fun to eat, and oh so easy to prepare. You can find them in the dried pasta section, usually packaged in a small box.

I cup acini di pepe pasta
2 tablespoons unsalted butter
2 tablespoons freshly squeezed lemon juice
I tablespoon minced fresh flat-leaf parsley
2 tablespoons chopped oven-roasted tomatoes (*page 158*)
½ cup sugar snap peas
Salt and freshly ground black pepper

1 In a large pot of salted boiling water, cook the pasta for 7 to 9 minutes, until al dente. Drain in a fine-mesh sieve and set aside.

2 In a skillet, melt the butter over medium heat. Stir in the lemon juice and parsley, then add the tomatoes and snap peas and cook for I minute, or just until heated through. Add the pasta, tossing to coat. Season with salt and pepper and serve at once.

Serves 4 as a side dish or light lunch

BROCCOLI RABE

his is broccoli for grown-ups: bitter, garlicky, and utterly addictive. Broccoli rabe (also known as rapini) is a staple in Italian cuisine; the florets are smaller and the stalks more tender than the broccoli commonly grown in American gardens. Its bitter edge is perfectly accented in this recipe by the olive oil and slivered garlic.

2 bunches broccoli rabe, cut into 2-inch pieces
2 tablespoons olive oil
4 cloves garlic, slivered
1 teaspoon red pepper flakes
½ lemon
Salt and freshly ground black pepper

1 Fill a bowl half full with ice cubes and add cold water to cover. In a saucepan of salted boiling water, cook the broccoli rabe for 3 to 4 minutes, until evenly dark and shiny and the leaves are wilted. Using a slotted spoon, transfer the broccoli rabe to the ice-water bath and let cool for 2 minutes. Transfer to paper towels to drain.

2 In a cast-iron skillet, heat the olive oil over medium-low heat. Add the garlic and sauté for 2 to 3 minutes, until golden. Add the red pepper flakes, then the broccoli rabe, and sauté for 2 to 3 minutes, or until crisp-tender. Squeeze the lemon over the top and toss to coat. Season with salt and pepper, remove from the heat, and serve immediately.

Serves 2 to 4

OVEN-ROASTED ASPARAGUS

he secret garlic cam at the Stinking Rose has captured diners picking up these asparagus spears and eating them with their bare hands! If that isn't shocking enough, you might be amazed to discover that these very same people walk out the door with huge smiles on their faces. Sinister, indeed.

2 pounds asparagus, trimmed

2 tablespoons extra-virgin olive oil

Salt and freshly ground black pepper

½ lemon

1 Preheat the oven to 400°F. Put the asparagus in a large baking dish and toss with the olive oil to lightly coat each spear. Season with salt and pepper. Roast until crisp-tender, 12 to 15 minutes, tossing once halfway through.

2 Transfer to a platter, sprinkle very lightly with juice from the lemon, and serve at once.

Serves 6

POLENTA WITH FONTINA CHEESE & HERBS

e hope you won't think we're being corny when we say that this recipe turns boring old polenta into a rich, creamy treat that can be served alongside any meat or fish dish.

4 cups chicken broth
1 clove garlic, minced
1 tablespoon minced fresh thyme
1 tablespoon minced fresh rosemary
1 cup polenta
1 tablespoon unsalted butter
1 cup (4 ounces) shredded Fontina cheese
Salt and freshly ground black pepper

1 In a heavy saucepan, heat the broth over medium-high heat until it comes to a boil. Add the garlic, thyme, and rosemary. Gradually add the polenta, whisking constantly to incorporate. Decrease the heat to medium-low and cook, stirring frequently, for about 20 minutes, or until thick and very creamy. Remove from the heat and stir in the butter and cheese until melted.

2 Season with salt and pepper and serve hot.

Serves 4

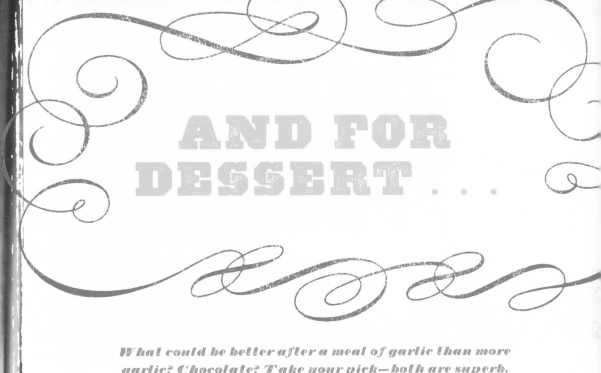

AND FOR DESSERT . . .

What could be better after a meal of garlic than more garlic? Chocolate? Take your pick—both are superb.

GARLIC ICE CREAM

You've heard the rumors, now try the real thing. It tastes a heck of a lot better than it sounds: think creamy vanilla ice cream with a hint of the roasty garlic sweetness. If you didn't know that the ice cream contained garlic, you might not even guess it was in there. Why not impress your guests at your next dinner party by whipping up a batch? It tastes even more decadent when drizzled with hot Mole Sauce (page 160).

2 cups whole milk

½ cup sugar

½ cup heavy cream

1½ tablespoons honey

2 tablespoons mashed roasted garlic cloves *(page 155)*

1 vanilla bean, halved lengthwise

7 large egg yolks

1 In a heavy saucepan, combine the milk, ¼ cup of the sugar, the cream, honey, and garlic and stir until blended. Using the flat edge of a butter knife, scrape the seeds from the vanilla bean into the milk mixture. Add the bean halves and stir. Bring the mixture to a boil over medium-high heat, stirring occasionally. Remove from the heat and cover to keep warm.

2 In a bowl, combine the remaining ¼ cup sugar and the egg yolks. Whisk for 2 to 3 minutes, until thick and pale in color.

☞ CONTINUED

3 Gradually whisk ½ cup of the hot milk mixture into the egg yolks in a thin stream. Gradually add the remaining milk mixture ½ cup at a time.

4 Pour the mixture into a saucepan and cook, stirring constantly, over medium-low heat until it coats the back of the spoon. Remove from the heat. Place the saucepan in a bowl of ice water and stir occasionally until it has reached room temperature, about 30 minutes.

5 Freeze in an ice cream maker according to the manufacturer's instructions. Eat right away for a soft-serve consistency, or transfer to a container and place in the freezer for 1 hour to harden.

Makes about 1 quart

CHOCOLATE WALNUT BROWNIE MARTINI MOUSSE

A t the Stinking Rose, we don't think that there can ever be too much of a good thing. Don't believe us? Just try this dessert. Inside of a giant martini glass, we alternate layers of thick, creamy chocolate mousse and smooth coffee mousse with crumbles of walnut brownies, and top it off with generous dollops of whipped cream. Chocolate, coffee, cream, and nuts . . . what could be more decadent?

BROWNIES

1¼ cups unsalted butter

12 ounces bittersweet chocolate, roughly chopped

1¼ cups unbleached white flour

1 teaspoon salt

6 large eggs

1 teaspoon vanilla extract

1½ cups white sugar

1¼ cups walnuts, roughly chopped

CHOCOLATE MOUSSE

½ cup (1 stick) unsalted butter

2 cups cold heavy cream

4 ounces bittersweet chocolate, grated or chopped

1 teaspoon vanilla extract

CONTINUED

4 egg whites

⅓ cup sugar

½ teaspoon cream of tartar

COFFEE MOUSSE

½ cup (1 stick) unsalted butter

1 cup cold heavy cream

½ cup strongly brewed coffee

4 egg whites

⅓ cup sugar

½ cup cold heavy cream

1 tablespoon sugar

Bittersweet chocolate shavings, for garnish

1 To make the brownies: preheat the oven to 350°F. Grease and flour a 9 by 13-inch baking dish.

2 In a heavy-bottomed saucepan, melt the butter together with the chocolate over low heat, stirring with a wooden spoon to prevent sticking. When the ingredients are fully melted and combined, about 8 minutes, remove from the heat.

3 In a large bowl, combine the flour with the salt. In a separate bowl, beat the eggs with the vanilla and sugar. Slowly pour the chocolate mixture into the egg mixture, beating with a whisk to combine. Pour the wet mixture into the flour and stir with a large wooden spoon until smooth. Add the walnuts.

☞ CONTINUED

4 Pour into the prepared baking dish and bake for about 25 minutes, or until a knife inserted in the center is sticky but not wet. Remove from the oven. When the brownies are cool, cut four 2-inch square pieces out of the pan and crumble, using your hands or a dull knife, into small pieces.

5 To make the chocolate mousse: Place the butter in a heavy-bottomed saucepan over medium heat. As the butter begins to melt, pour in the cream and stir with a wooden spoon to combine. As soon as the cream begins to bubble, which should take about 3 minutes, remove from the heat. Sprinkle the chocolate over the top and stir with a wooden spoon until the chocolate is thoroughly melted into the cream. Add the vanilla.

6 In a heatproof bowl, whisk the egg whites together with the cream of tartar and sugar. Using an electric mixer at medium-high speed, whip the egg whites over until soft peaks form. Slowly pour the lukewarm chocolate cream into the egg whites, whisking vigorously to combine. Place the bowl over a pan of gently boiling water and stir gently, cooking for about 4 minutes to cook the eggs through. Remove from the hot-water bath and let cool to room temperature. Cover with plastic wrap and refrigerate for at least 4 hours, until the mousse is firm.

7 To make the coffee mousse: Place the butter in a heavy-bottomed saucepan over medium heat. As the butter begins to melt, pour in the cream and stir with a wooden spoon to combine. As soon as the cream begins to bubble, which should take about 3 minutes, remove from the heat. Add the coffee and stir to incorporate.

8 In a heatproof bowl, whisk the egg whites together with the sugar. Using an electric mixer at medium-high speed, whip the egg whites until soft peaks form. Slowly pour the lukewarm coffee cream into the egg whites, whisking vigorously to combine. Place the bowl over a pan of gently boiling water and stir gently for about 4 minutes to cook the eggs through. Remove from the hot-water bath and let cool to room temperature. Cover with plastic wrap and refrigerate for at least 4 hours, until the mousse is firm.

9 To assemble the dessert: Scoop ¼ cup of the coffee mousse into an oversize martini glass or 16-ounce parfait glass. Scatter a tablespoon of crumbled brownie bits on top, then place ¼ cup of the chocolate mousse over the brownies. Repeat the layers until the top of the glass is reached. Fill another three glasses in the same manner. Cover with plastic wrap and chill for at least two hours, or up to 48 hours, before serving.

10 Just before serving, whip the ½ cup cream in a cold bowl until soft peaks form. Add the 1 tablespoon sugar and whisk to incorporate.

11 Remove the plastic wrap from the glasses and top with generous dollops of whipped cream. Garnish with chocolate shavings and serve with leftover brownies on the side.

Serves 4

BITS AND PIECES

We put all the recipes that don't fit neatly into one of the other sections right here, from roasted garlic to mole sauce.

GARLIC CHIPS

G arlic has often been called an aphrodisiac, and here at the Stinking Rose, we affectionately refer to our crisp garlic chips as the "poor man's Viagra"—and we sprinkle them everywhere! Far from being overwhelmingly "garlicky," they add a mellow, roasted sweetness and nice crunch wherever they appear. In order to make good chips, the slices must be paper-thin; we highly recommend the use of a mandoline, which can be found at most kitchen supply stores.

> 4 to 5 large bulbs elephant garlic (see note)
> 3 cups whole milk
> Vegetable oil, for deep-frying

1 Separate the cloves from the garlic bulbs and cut off the hard end of each clove where it was connected to the bulb. Drop the cloves into boiling water for 30 seconds, then drain and peel by squeezing the cloves.

2 Using a mandoline or a very sharp paring knife, create a pile of ultra-thin, chiplike slices.

3 In a heavy saucepan, combine 1 cup of the milk and the garlic slices. Bring just to a boil over medium heat; immediately remove from the heat and drain through a sieve. Repeat twice. (This is called the "sweetening blanch," and it removes the bitterness and strong alkaline taste from the garlic.) Transfer the drained garlic to paper towels to dry.

4 In a large, heavy skillet, heat 1 to 2 inches of oil over high heat to 375°F; it should be hot and bubbly.

5 Working in small batches, drop the garlic slices into the oil and fry until golden brown and crisp, about 1 minute. They cook very fast, so do not walk away from the stove! Using a slotted spoon, transfer the chips to paper towels to drain and cool completely.

6 Use now, or store in an airtight container in a cool, dry place for up to 1 month.

Makes about 1½ cups

NOTE

Elephant garlic is the mellowest variety. Its large cloves are far easier to peel than those of smaller varieties.

GARLIC COMPOUND BUTTER

For centuries, cooks have always said that butter makes it better! We'd just like to add a tiny addendum to that saying: garlic butter makes it better! From shellfish to veggies, nearly every savory dish becomes that much tastier with a drizzle of this lovely stuff.

> 2 cloves garlic, diced
> 1 tablespoon small capers
> Juice of ½ lemon
> 2 tablespoons dry white wine
> ¼ cup unsalted butter, at room temperature

1 In a small saucepan over low heat, combine all the ingredients and whisk until melted and thoroughly blended. Pour into a ramekin.

2 Use now, or cover and refrigerate for up to 1 week. Melt over low heat just before serving.

Makes about ½ cup

ROASTED GARLIC CLOVES

If there was one item from this cookbook that you were to incorporate into your daily cooking routine—and we hope that there are more than that—but if you could choose only one, we hope this would be it. Roasted garlic cloves are sweet and nutty, and they impart a wonderful flavor to every dish that they meet. If you haven't had the pleasure of cooking with them before, please don't delay..

      2 cups garlic cloves
      I cup olive oil

1 In a heavy saucepan, combine the garlic and olive oil and cook over low heat for about 40 minutes, stirring once at 20 minutes, until the garlic begins to soften. Preheat the oven to 250°F. Using a slotted spoon, transfer the garlic to a baking sheet. Bake for 25 to 30 minutes, until the cloves are golden brown and slightly wrinkled.

Makes about ½ cup

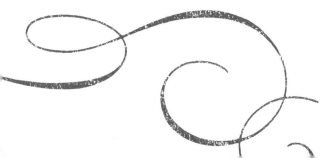

ROASTED GARLIC BULBS 👉

Check out these bulbs! Roasted garlic bulbs are a beautiful way to serve garlic at a dinner party—the garlic is so soft that it can be spread on bread or toast with a butter knife. We recommend elephant garlic for this recipe, since the cloves are so big, but any garlic will work just fine.

> 3 large bulbs garlic
> ¾ cup water
> 1½ teaspoons white wine vinegar
> 2 tablespoons extra-virgin olive oil

1 Preheat the oven to 350°F. With a very sharp knife, cut the tips (about ½ inch) off the top of the bulb in one slice, so that the tops of the cloves are exposed. Remove the loosest papery layers. Pour the water and vinegar into a small baking dish and place the garlic bulbs in the center. Drizzle the olive oil over the exposed tops of the cloves, then cover with aluminum foil. Roast for about 1 hour, or until the garlic is very soft when poked and the outer papery layers are crisp.

Makes about 1 cup

OVEN-ROASTED TOMATOES 👉

e love oven-roasted tomatoes. They taste like candy, so sweet and delicious that we add them to all kinds of dishes. Try making a batch and tossing them into a salad; serve them on an antipasto platter alongside olives and cheese and cured meats; cut them into ribbons and stir them into your scrambled eggs. You might even find yourself eating them plain, like we do!

1½ pounds Roma tomatoes, halved lengthwise
2 tablespoons olive oil
2 tablespoons chopped fresh basil
1 teaspoon minced garlic
Salt and freshly ground black pepper

1 Preheat the oven to 225°F. Put the tomato halves in a bowl and toss with the olive oil, basil, and garlic to coat thoroughly. Season with salt and pepper.

2 Arrange in a single layer on a baking sheet and bake for 45 minutes to 1 hour, until the tomatoes are shriveled to about two-thirds their original size; they should still be soft to the touch. Do not allow the edges to become crisp. Remove and let cool.

3 Use now, or store in an airtight container in the refrigerator for up to 3 weeks.

Makes about 1 cup

ROASTED GARLIC & BASIL AIOLI

id you know that Nero is said to have invented aioli? We don't know why the history of garlic is populated with so many scandalous figures, but when you want just a hint of garlic for a sandwich or roasted veggies, this aioli is the perfect choice. Note that since it does contain raw eggs, it should not be eaten by pregnant women or individuals with compromised health.

1 bulb roasted garlic *(page 156)*
3 large egg yolks
¼ cup chopped fresh basil
1 teaspoon coarse sea salt or kosher salt
1 tablespoon freshly squeezed lemon juice
¾ cup extra-virgin olive oil
Freshly ground black pepper

1 Hold the roasted garlic bulb over a blender or food processor and squeeze gently to extract all of the garlic from the skin. Add the egg yolks, basil, salt, and lemon juice and pulse until well blended and smooth.

2 With the machine running, very gradually add the oil, first in drops, then in a thin stream, and process until creamy and thick. Season with salt and pepper.

3 Use now, or cover and refrigerate for up to 3 days.

Makes 1 cup

MOLE SAUCE 👉

L ike your mother's bread recipe or your grandmother's famous eggnog, there are more versions for mole sauce than can possibly be counted. Everyone has a different interpretation of this dark, intense sauce. Ours incorporates the distinctive kick of garlic, which gives it a flavor that we think borders on sublime. Holy mole! This is one tasty sauce!

1 yellow onion, chopped

3 cloves garlic, halved

Olive oil, for drizzling

2 ancho chiles

4 pasilla chiles

½ cup chicken broth

1 tablespoon distilled white vinegar

2 tablespoons dark molasses

½ teaspoon ground cinnamon

½ teaspoon ground coriander

½ teaspoon ground cloves

2 tablespoons heavy cream

2 ounces bittersweet chocolate, chopped

1 Preheat the oven to 350°F. Spread the onion and garlic on a baking sheet and drizzle with olive oil. Roast for 20 to 25 minutes, until the garlic is golden brown and the onion is curling and browned on the edges.

2 Meanwhile, soak the chiles in warm water for at least 30 minutes, or until rehydrated. Stem and seed the chiles, then rinse and pat them dry. Chop coarsely. In a blender, combine the chiles and the roasted garlic and onions and pulse until a thick paste is formed. Add the chicken broth, vinegar, molasses, cinnamon, coriander, and cloves and purée until smooth.

3 Pour into a small saucepan and stir in the cream. Bring to a simmer over medium heat, then stir in the chocolate until melted; do not boil. Cook, stirring frequently, for about 3 minutes to blend the flavors. Remove from the heat and serve warm.

Makes about 1 cup

PIZZA DOUGH

 n Italy, everyone has a special way of working the dough to create the perfect crust. We've developed a recipe that is simple and fun. It makes enough dough for 4 pizzettes and each of the recipes on pages 135 through 143 are enough for 2 pizzettes.

1 cup warm water (105° to 115°F)
1 package active dry yeast (2¼ teaspoons)
1 teaspoon sugar
1 teaspoon salt
2¼ to 2½ cups unbleached all-purpose flour
1 tablespoon cornmeal

1 Pour the water into a small bowl, sprinkle the yeast and sugar over and whisk to blend. Let stand until foamy, about 10 minutes. (If the mixture doesn't foam, discard and start over with new yeast.)

2 In a large bowl, stir the salt and 1½ cups of the flour together. Add the yeast mixture and stir to blend with a heavy spoon. Add the remaining flour in ¼-cup increments until the dough clings together into a ball.

3 On a floured work surface, with floured hands, knead the dough for 7 to 8 minutes, until smooth, soft, and elastic, reflouring when the dough becomes too sticky.

4 Divide the dough into 4 pieces and form into balls. Place the balls on a lightly oiled baking sheet and cover with a cloth. Set in a warm place until doubled in size. Punch down gently; the dough is ready to shape for pizzettes.

Makes dough for 4 pizzettes

PASTA DOUGH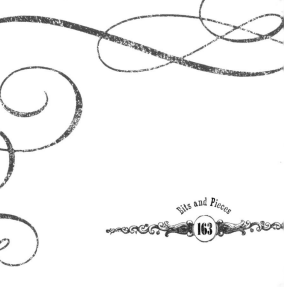

If you're lucky enough to have a pasta machine, you already know how much fun it can be to make your own pasta. If you haven't tried it yet, there's no time like right now to get started! Once you've made fresh pasta, you'll agree that it simply doesn't compare to the dried stuff. It's in a league all of its own. For the best results, be sure to follow the instructions that come with your pasta machine when rolling out the dough.

> 2½ cups semolina or bread flour
>
> 1 teaspoon salt
>
> 4 large eggs
>
> 2 tablespoons extra-virgin olive oil

1 In a large mixing bowl, stir together the flour and salt. With the back of a large spoon, make a deep indentation in the middle of the flour, so that it looks like a crater. Add the eggs and olive oil into the crater and use your hands to gently incorporate the wet and dry ingredients. Form the dough into a ball and place it on a lightly floured surface. Knead for 6 to 8 minutes, until smooth and elastic adding flour as necessary to keep the dough from sticking. The dough should not be at all sticky, but should feel silky. Wrap in plastic wrap and let stand at room temperature for at least 15 minutes before rolling out with a pasta machine or a rolling pin.

2 Use now, or cover and refrigerate for up to 1 day.

Makes 1 pound

INDEX